BRITAIN'S 100
EXTRAORDINARY
GOLF HOLES

GEOFF HARVEY & VANESSA STROWGER

AP
AESCULUS
PRESS LTD

An Aesculus Press Book

Managing Editor – David Ikerrin

Editors – Anna Middleton, Diane Dekuysscher and Romilly Evans

Principal Photographers – Adam Godfrey and Mark Davidson Fildes

Thanks to the following for their tremendous support – Chris Golden, Peter Greenhalgh

Design concept
Wheelhouse Creative Ltd
www.wheelhousecreative.co.uk

Layout and typesetting
Mouse House Print Shop
The Barn, Bath Place, Hale, Cheshire

First published in Great Britain in 2003, reprinted 2006
By Aesculus Press Limited, 8 Peacock Yard, Iliffe Street
London, SE17 3LH
www.bestbetbooks.com

CONTENTS

INTRODUCTION

The idea of compiling a collection of Britain's most extraordinary golf holes was not sparked at one of the prestigious Open courses, but at the 6th tee at *Woodkirk Valley Golf and County Club,* Tingley, a tiny pastureland layout in West Yorkshire. Playing in 1993, the course seemed to finish after five holes. Stuck at the corner of a field, it was impossible to tell where the 6th green might be – or if it existed at all. One of us had the bright idea of clambering down a tree-lined slope where, to his amazement, he discovered a dell with a series of streams, bits of old farmyard machinery and…a small green.

Actually to play the hole required a team effort, utilising shouts and hand-signals. With no other players in sight, we took turns at firing seven-irons over the trees and into the gorge for about half and hour until we managed to find the green. Though it had taken about 30 balls, we were happy to have 'tamed' what we imagined to be Britain's most amazing golf hole. Over a decade later, the course

has now been rearranged, robbing us of the chance to easily complete one percent of our collection.

'Britain's 100 Extraordinary Golf Holes' is a mixture of the scenic, the awe-inspiring and the odd; the steepest, the longest, the shortest and the humpiest; holes with buildings, roads, monuments and sheep in play; spectacular ravines, impossible carries, gorges and cliffs; and with plenty of water and gigantic bunkers thrown in.

The criteria for inclusion were always rather difficult to define. At its most basic, we were looking for holes where, at some point along the route from the tee, the player would stare in amazement at the scene that greeted him – beyond that it is difficult to be more precise. Our selection makes no claim to feature the most 'difficult' holes, though some of them happen to be bordering on the impossible

for a player of anything less than average ability. The term 'signature hole' is used to describe a course's 'best'. This tends to be the one that poses the most interesting technical challenge. As a mainly photographic project, however, we were always somewhat keener on strong visual features as opposed to the subtle intricacies of a hole.

When we seriously began researching the book, it was apparent that many players struggle to remember the details of interesting golf holes that they have played; rather like digging for long-lost subconscious material. Such is the artificial mental intensity of a round of golf that, when actually playing, you don't always take in much about the course in general. Who really cares about the magnificent view to the medieval castle on the peninsula to the north when you're wedged into the lip of the bunker from hell?

Thinking about holes we had played, it seemed strange that at the time we didn't really take in their unique features. It was only when we had played *Altrincham*, Cheshire, a number of times that we realised how intriguing the 16th was since we always seemed to find ourselves ploughing through a dark thicket, only to end up in a river. And what was that 80ft pit in the middle of the 17th fairway?

Unlike many golf books, 'Britain's 100 Extraordinary Golf Holes' does not actually require readers to do anything. Pick up most golf publications and there is an implicit understanding that we must jump into action, improve our putting style,

or brush up on hazard visualisation. We would be very interested to hear of anyone who claims to have played all 100 that feature here but the main thrust of our collection is, first and foremost, entertainment.

Initially, the idea was to try and present a 'formal' Top 100 of Britain's most extraordinary holes listed in reverse order. The problem we immediately stumbled across was what could loosely be described as 'The Beatles' phenomena. If you try and compile a Top 100 of anything, it gets clogged up with a small number of contributors monopolising many of the positions. A few courses are so packed

with features that, within a 'strict' Top 100, you would find the same names cropping up again and again. *Painswick*, Gloucestershire, a fascinating course playing across the public land of the Cotswold Way, could have probably filled five of a 'proper' Top 10. The amazing *Shiskine*, Isle of Arran, might account for the remaining places with *Manor House*, Wiltshire, hot on its heels.

To prevent certain courses dominating, each of our 100 comes from a different course. The 100 are presented in alphabetical order – with their rank number appearing in the little golf ball above the name. The pages are also colour-coded by rank so you will recognise the Top 20 quickly as they all appear on a yellow background, the next 20 on a green background and so on as indicated below.

The ranking is not to be taken too seriously, as it will always be subjective as to why one hole is more extraordinary than another. However, the authors had no part in the ranking process, mainly because we realised we had developed quite a strong bias towards the clubs that had been particularly helpful in the course of our research, in which case some Yorkshire, Welsh and remote Scottish courses might have been artificially 'promoted'. Instead, all the material was put to a panel of golfers, of differing abilities, who independently reviewed and ranked each hole without any interference, bribes or coercion!

We have limited ourselves to England, Scotland and Wales simply to keep the project reasonably manageable. We hope to cover both Northern and Southern Ireland in a separate volume in the future. There is a reasonable geographical spread between the regions, with one glaring exception: we are short on Welsh courses. Wales is one of the unjustifiably 'lost' golfing areas. However, the courses in Wales are generally very keen to attract visitors and, as such, make a good venue for a golf holiday. For those of you interested in the geographical spread of the courses, these are shown altogether on a map on page 213.

The knotty subject of how amenable clubs are to visitors cannot go without comment. British golf is mostly played at private clubs. Some survive financially on a relatively small number of members sometimes paying huge fees. With only a proportion of members playing regularly, these courses can remain virtually empty most of the year and they put little effort into attracting visitors. Others are commercially 'geared-up' and rely heavily on visitors boosting the coffers. The authors got the general impression that clubs with websites were clearly interested in attracting visitors and tended to fall into the 'friendly' category.

Like many areas of sport and leisure, golf will have to start actively marketing itself to younger people for all Britain's courses to stay in the black. Golf does not get as much terrestrial TV coverage as it did and no matter how attractive the game, a grumpy club captain is no match for the draw of football and the commercial attentions of the likes of Sony and Nintendo.

It was always our intention to try and showcase some courses that did not constantly feature on TV and in the golfing press. There are plenty of hole-by-hole accounts of the great British links courses but the small number of Championship courses tend to dominate discussions to the exclusion of others. The fact that the British Open is always, by tradition, played on a links course means that terrestrial TV only features a small and quite specialised selection of British clubs. On our golfing tour of Britain, we found it fascinating that some clubs are quite well-known to golfers generally, whereas others, of perhaps equal status, are almost delightfully anonymous. The craggy delights of *Cruden Bay* are comparatively well-publicised.

However, the incredible moonscape of nearby *Cullen* rarely gets a mention. Similarly, the opening drive over the sea at *Machrihanish* is the stuff of legends but mention the unbelievable 6th at *Eyemouth* and you get mostly quizzical looks.

The process of compiling the book was based on a mixture of trawling golf publications, clubs' internet as well as specialist sites, word of mouth and inviting clubs themselves to submit holes. We first narrowed down the 3,500 British Clubs to 800 'possibles'. Sometimes we had specific information. On other occasions we had only the vaguest idea that they had a feature of interest. In keeping with the phenomena that it is not always possible to spot something right in front of you, many club secretaries could not conceive that their course contained an extraordinary feature. It became something of a ritual that upon contacting a course, they would initially deny any knowledge of what interested us. So we often had to press them with a few details. For example, 'Isn't it the case that the 4th at your course features a 200ft drop over white water rapids to the smallest green in the world?' Finally there would usually be a flicker of recognition.

We know that we have probably missed out clubs and features that are just as interesting as the ones included here. With around 65,000 golf holes in the UK we do not claim to have considered every single one, only a fraction that hit us in the face. We decided we had finished the research when, on talking to a few particularly well-travelled players, we realised that we had already considered all the dozen or so courses they mentioned. We hope readers will note omissions in a reasonably charitable

frame of mind. Of Britain's major courses, the most notable absences are probably the 10th at *The De Vere Belfry* and the 'Postage Stamp' 12th at *Royal Troon*.

We have tried to find a balance between classic and, what some might call, trivial or undesirable features. After much debate we decided not to feature a hole with an electricity pylon in the middle. Though pylons make for interesting unnatural hazards we eventually felt that other courses might baulk at the idea of being up against bits of the national grid. We are, therefore, particularly grateful to clubs who had no qualms about letting us feature some of the stranger oddities – for instance, *Orsett*, with its protectively clad cottage.

There are holes we are still struggling to find. Is there really a course in central Wales where golfers have to shin up a rope to the green? This was a persistent rumour, though we are not sure whether it is actually true – so if anyone knows the definitive answer... In fact, we would welcome any suggestions, stories and, to a point, constructive moans for future editions.

69

ABERNETHY

NETHY BRIDGE,
HIGHLAND,
PH25 3EB

2ND
'CASTLE ROY'
PAR 3 - 115 YARDS

A VARIETY OF HAZARDS ON THE SHORT PAR-THREE 2ND

Our collection starts with a hazard-packed short hole at this traditional Highland course. The 2nd squeezes in just about every conceivable obstacle in the 115 yards between tee and green. From a slightly raised position you need to hit over a pond, a path, a boggy area, the first fence, a minor road, the second fence, avoid three bunkers and onto the two-tiered green. Anyone hooking their first shot could end up on or over another road, the B970. This majestic area of the Scottish Highlands doesn't experience a rush-hour as such, so players are rarely kept waiting by queues of traffic.

Abernethy's 8th fairway (246 yards, par-four) is home to an imposing 25ft war memorial. For golfers this is quite handy, as the 8th would otherwise be blind, making the memorial a convenient marker post. Bearing in mind it is what everyone aims for, it is subject to an unusually generous ruling. Anyone hitting the monument (a very frequent occurrence) gets to retake their shot without a penalty.

Adding to the dubious tradition of naming British regions after TV programmes that were filmed there, Nethy Bridge has been dubbed 'Monarch Country' as it was a major location in the BBC's 'Monarch of the Glen' drama series.

———

Galashiels, Borders, has a number of relics from the Second World War in play. Stone cairns are dotted around the course, with one on the 13th fairway itself. Less ancient than they look, they were constructed to prevent enemy planes from landing on the flat area at the top of the hill.

ABERNETHY – WAR MEMORIAL ON THE 8TH

THE MEMORIAL MAKES A CONVENIENT MARKER POST

CAIRN AT GALASHIELS

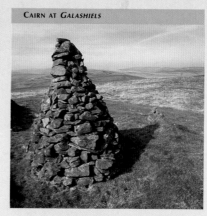

ABERNETHY – LOOKING BACK UP THE 8TH FAIRWAY

THE ADDINGTON

CROYDON,
SURREY,
CRO 5AB

13TH
PAR 3 - 230 YARDS

The Addington has the look and feel of a course in the wilds of the Scottish Highlands, with its colourful heather, rustic bridges and rather ill-defined bunkers – which makes it even more surprising that it is actually only a few minutes from East Croydon railway station in South London. The course's unique flavour is aided by the fact that the layout is largely as it was on the death of the designer J F Abercromby in 1935. It is one of those courses where it is difficult to pick a signature hole. The picture-book 13th plays over rhododendrons from an elevated tee. Players cross over the remains of a chalk pit via a trestle bridge.

Just prior to its opening in 1917, The Addington's layout was

THE TREE-LINED 13TH OVER RHODODENDRONS

subject to a last-minute change of plan. The original clubhouse was constructed out of ex-army huts intended for a site at the top of a hill. However, horses were unable to pull them up the slope so they had to stay where they were behind the current 15th green, meaning the holes needed to be hastily renumbered to accommodate the wrongly positioned clubhouse.

The Addington's 17th plays over a ravine with another of the courses' characteristic bridges enabling players to cross to the green.

The 6th features a 30ft bunker so fierce that P G Wodehouse once wrote a letter "c/o bunker at the 6th, Addington Golf Club". More recently during filming of a Discovery channel documentary, ex-Goodie, Tim Brooke-Taylor, took six shots to escape from it.

The course has its own resident night-time security system. The peacocks that live in the trees do not take kindly to being disturbed and react to intruders by emitting a frightful screeching noise. The Addington was completed during the First World War and remained virtually unplayed until the end of hostilities. To this day, it has a reputation for rarely being busy, strange considering its London location.

THE ADDINGTON – GORSE-FILLED RAVINE AT THE 17TH

88

ALDWICKBURY PARK

HARPENDEN,
HERTFORDSHIRE,
AL5 1AB

12TH
PAR 4 - 440 YARDS

PLAYING OVER THE **12TH'S** HEDGE

Opened in 1995, *Aldwickbury Park* is a parkland golfing oasis within the Hertfordshire suburbs. The hazard on the 12th of the Park Course is not entirely intentional. At 220 yards from the tee lies a 5-6ft hedge that runs across the fairway providing a fairly stiff challenge to long-hitters and the prospect of getting stuck immediately behind it for everyone else. The designers had not intended on keeping it as a feature, but it was discovered that planning regulations prevented it from being removed – a sort of 'listed hedge'.

ALDWICKBURY PARK – 12TH TEE

Golf Clubs are frequently embroiled in minor planning niggles, but *Moorend*, Cheshire, has had to endure a particularly protracted battle with a water company over the land of its nine-hole pay-and-play course. Owner Peter Holmes received a letter from United Utilities in 1997 saying it wanted to lay a giant pipe. The work, which involved a 4ft wide trench, did little to improve the looks of the maturing course, causing players to stay away. Five years later, Mr Holmes received £5,000 compensation, but calculated he was worse off overall to the tune of £140,000.

ALDWICKBURY PARK'S HEDGE HAS A MAGNETIC ATTRACTION TO GOLF BALLS

BAILDON

WEST YORKSHIRE,
BD17 5PP

2ND
'QUARRY HOLE'
PAR 3 - 177 YARDS

2ND OVER THE ROCKY CHASM

It is with some understatement that the high point on Baildon Moor, half a mile west of the 2nd hole, is called Windy Hill. The area around Ilkley is renowned for its biting cold, and after posing on the 2nd tee for five minutes at 8am one spring morning, the author scurried back to the car muttering about the chill. Members are made of sterner stuff.

The 2nd tee looks out onto a chasm of rock. With the westerly wind full in the face, most opt for a fairway wood. Bingley Road, running across the moor to the left, is out of bounds and anything right can get swallowed up in a deep hollow. In common with other courses with vertical drops in play, the 2nd comes with a painted warning at the front of the teeing area.

Unusually for an inland course, there are no trees at *Baildon* – and almost no bunkers. Over the years, the rough has been trimmed back, but still poses a significant threat on most fairways. The course is set out on common land, with horses, sheep and the occasional deer going about their business. Families looking for a nice spot have been known to set out picnics on the fairways. Despite its apparent remoteness, the club is only a stiff walk from the urban area of Shipley, with the city of Bradford lying to the south. Potential visitors should check out the club's excellent website, www.baildongolfclub.com with its unnerving descriptions: e.g. '8th, 397 yards – Deviationists are severely punished'.

BRAMSHAW – PLAY AROUND THE PONIES

TAPED GREEN AT *ROYAL NORTH DEVON*

Horses feature most prominently on the Hampshire courses of *Bramshaw* and *New Forest*. The wild ponies seem oblivious to golfers and often need to be encouraged to move out of the line of fire. The closely mown grass of golf greens is of little culinary interest to cattle. But they love to rub themselves against flagpoles, causing some British clubs to take action to keep them off putting surfaces. *Royal North Devon's* greens are surrounded with lengths of tape to keep animals away.

BAMBURGH CASTLE

BAMBURGH,
NORTHUMBERLAND,
NE69 7DE

8TH 'ISLAND'
PAR 3 - 164 YARDS

A hole named 'Island' naturally conjures up an image of a green surrounded by water. But the island green here is surrounded by rock. The par-three plays across a grass gully up a granite face to an uncomfortably small putting area. The rocks account for anything short, right or long from the tee – and there is not much room for manoeuvre on the left either. Pitching directly onto them is definitely not recommended as the ball can ricochet off at any angle – and great speed!

PLAYING ONTO THE ROCKY ISLAND OF THE 8TH

BAMBURGH CASTLE – 8TH WITH THE BACKDROP OF THE NORTHUMBERLAND COAST

Bamburgh Castle has more than its fair share of amazing holes, including a heart-stopping 182-yard opener, 'The Dinkie', played across a gaping chasm. Bamburgh Castle itself, visible from much of the course, featured in 'El Cid' and more recently in 'Prince of Thieves' starring Kevin Costner before his 'Tin Cup' days. The Holy Island of Lindisfarne is also visible – in fact, from the 15th you can see four castles on a clear day.

The course certainly breeds loyalty amongst its staff with the current quartet of greenkeepers, led by George Milliken, boasting 50 years service between them. *Piltdown*, East Sussex has a similar claim to fame: the current professional, Jason Partridge, is only the third in the club's 100 year history. With 14 years service, he is just a probationer compared to his two predecessors, with 51 years and 37 years service respectively.

BAMBURGH CASTLE

BARRA

ISLE OF BARRA,
WESTERN ISLES,
HS9 5YQ

4TH
'CNOC NA FHITHICH'
PAR 4 – 318 YARDS

The British Isles' most remote golf course lies on the Hebridean Island of Barra. A complete round trip is just 12 miles. The short nine-hole layout is on velvety machair turf, ideal for golf. But the land-ownership issues in the region mean that players share their round with a variety of livestock, in *Barra's* case, herds of cows and hundreds of sheep. Crofting and golf compete, with the compromise that landowners graze their animals on the course and the club takes defensive measures to protect its greens. At *Barra*, this means solid post fencing with a wire mesh around each of the nine mostly square greens. Access to each is through a sturdy gate. The 4th has the most dramatic aspect, skirting the bay with the Borve Hills in the background.

Barra has an obscure footnote in British comedy history. When 'Dad's

THE 4TH – A CASE FOR BEING THE COUNTRY'S MOST REMOTE GOLF HOLE

Army' writers Croft and Perry devised the series, they wrote mock biographies of all the characters to aid script development. Private Fraser, the cynical Scottish undertaker played by Jon Lawrie, was said to have been a fisherman on the Isle of Barra before his National Service.

THE HEAVILY FORTIFIED 7TH AT *BARRA*

on common grazing land at *Sollas*, North Unst that cannot be found in any of the usual British golfing directories.

Like many of Britain's isolated courses, *Barra* is often unmanned. Visitors can turn up at any time and deposit their daily green fee in an honesty box.

The clubhouse at Hebridean neighbours, *Stornoway*, Isle of Lewis, is almost impossible to find as it has been deliberately built into a hill so as not to obstruct the views from the road. Nick Faldo visited *Scarista*, South Harris, and dutifully placed his fiver in the honesty box. Although finances at the Hebridean clubs tend to be tight, the note was collected, framed and mounted and is now the prize in the members' annual competition.

Many clubs take even more drastic action to discourage livestock. A number of British courses have electric fences around greens, notably *Brora*, Highland, where golfers have the company of ever-present cattle. Electric fences should not harm even the most inquisitive or careless of golfers, though their effect on those fitted with pacemakers can be problematic. The Hebrides have a number of 'unofficial' courses which the golfing completist should consider, including one built by locals

BRITAIN'S MOST REMOTE GOLF COURSE

74

BATH

SOMERSET,
BA2 6JG

14TH

PAR 3 - 154 YARDS

OVER THE EARTHWORKS AT THE 14TH

BATH – GO FOR IT OVER THE PRACTICE GROUND OR TAKE THE LONGER FAIRWAY ROUTE ON THE **17**TH

BATH'S STRANGELY UNDULATING **17**TH FAIRWAY

Bath is not a name that quickly springs to mind when thinking of the country's most ancient golfing tracts but the club was founded in 1880, making it the sixth oldest in the country. *Bath* has two feature holes, the first being the 154-yard, par-three 14th. From the front tee at 127 yards, it is a relatively painless short-iron across the rough-filled, fence-lined Wandsdyke earthworks. But the back tee needs another 30-yard carry and is somewhat more daunting.

A classic golfing dare confronts players at *Bath's* par-four 17th. The club has many features common to Britain's oldest clubs, particularly in the case of this hole where a stone wall challenges you to cut the corner over out of bounds. The wall and the fairway form a vast semi-circle of 310 yards but, if you don't feel like taking the longer route, it is 250 yards straight over the wall to the right of the tee, over the club's practice ground and, with a bit of luck, back over the wall to end up somewhere in the vicinity of the green. Giving this fairway a miss entirely can also have its advantages. The 60 yards before the green have some of the most peculiar terrain you can find on an English golf course – a series of formless humps ready to swallow up anything and everything.

62

BIGBURY

BIGBURY-ON-SEA,
DEVON,
TQ7 4BB

16TH
PAR 4 - 291 YARDS

THE ROUTE OVER THE WALL

Bigbury's 16th is possibly the ultimate example of a drive over out of bounds. Unless you actually see others playing the hole, the direct route to the 16th green is not an obvious option. Played 'properly', you are supposed to hit an iron up the fairway to the right of the wall, and then take a 90 degree left turn for your approach shot to the green. The green hugs the wall closely 150 yards further down its length. If the hole came early in the round many would probably choose the long way round. But why not live the dream and go straight over the field? At a full 250-yard carry, some are tempted to try and clear the far wall – but it takes an almighty blow to be successful.

This area of South Devon was particularly hard-hit by the foot-and-mouth outbreak in 2002. At any other time, players nipping into adjacent fields to collect stray shots may have been tolerated; if not encouraged, but during the dark days of the epidemic, golfers on many courses were issued dire warnings about encroaching onto farmland.

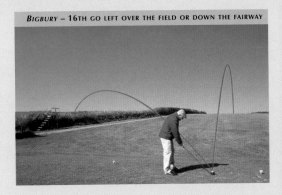

BIGBURY – 16TH GO LEFT OVER THE FIELD OR DOWN THE FAIRWAY

Bigbury's opening 455-yard par-four sweeps parallel to the B3392 road. Players are not allowed to tee-off when a car is approaching – but with the constant holiday traffic in the summer, this does not leave many windows of opportunity. It is not as if motorists don't have enough to worry about already in South Devon. Many of the single roads around Bigbury-on-Sea are bordered on both sides by very high hedges, making passing oncoming cars nerve-wracking for the area's many visitors. Through experience the locals have an uncanny appreciation of the precise width of their vehicles, allowing them to career around the lanes without too many scrapes.

BIGBURY – OPENING ROAD HOLE

BIGBURY – BURGH ISLAND FROM THE 15TH GREEN

NO TROLLEYS ON THE TEES
●
PLAYERS COMING ONTO THE 1ST TEE FROM THE 18TH GREEN TO ALTERNATE WITH PLAYERS STARTING ON THE 1ST TEE
●
Players MUST NOT drive off when a car is approaching

BIGBURY – ROAD WARNING

Bigbury's 14th tee must rank amongst the most scenic on the south coast, perched high above the Avon estuary. At the 15th green the panorama opens up to include the tiny Burgh Island, setting for Agatha Christie's 'And Then There Were None'.

The island is only reachable at high tide by a tractor.

87

BOXMOOR

HEMEL HEMPSTEAD,
HERTFORDSHIRE,
HP3 0DJ

3RD 'BURYWOOD'
PAR 3 - 188 YARDS

One way of assessing the difficulty of a par-three is to look at the frequency of holes-in-one. In a professional tournament there is about a 40% chance that an ace will be achieved, possibly much higher than might intuitively be guessed at.

One British par-three that has not seen its fair share of celebrations is *Boxmoor*, Hertfordshire. The 3rd plays sharply uphill, posing the classic problem that players invariably underestimate what it takes to reach the top. *Boxmoor's* 3rd went 100 years without ever having a hole-in-one and has still never been aced in stroke-play competition.

> THIS PAR-THREE WENT 100 YEARS WITHOUT EVER HAVING A HOLE-IN-ONE

THE SHARP INCLINE OF THE 3RD

To visualise the expected frequency of holes-in-one, imagine a large number of golfers striking a ball from the tee simultaneously causing the green to be peppered with balls. How many shots should it take before a single ball finds its way into the hole? Assuming the players are club-standard amateurs, we might expect it to take around 3,000 strikes. During a year a hole might be played 10,000 times, suggesting that an average par-three might be aced three times.

BOXMOOR – FEW MAKE IT ONTO THE 3RD GREEN IN ONE

BOXMOOR – 3RD TEE

Brother of the current secretary of *Boxmoor*, Bob Newark, had the ultimate put-down for the then secretary of the club, who, on seeing that he appeared to be teeing off from a position forward of the marker, asked testily 'Are you aware of the rules of golf?' Bob replied, 'No, but I'm a quick learner.' The secretary inquired why in that case his ball was in front of the designated area. 'That's easy' said the relieved golfer. 'I'm playing my second shot.'

BRANCEPETH CASTLE

**BRANCEPETH VILLAGE,
COUNTY DURHAM,
DH7 8EA**

9TH

PAR 3 - 207 YARDS

Constructed on what was Brancepeth Castle's deer park, this course has seven of its 18 holes playing over vast wooded ravines hidden in which are a number of golfer-unfriendly streams and the paths of the castle's former gardens. One of these carries on the 9th is considered so difficult that it has been nominated by an American golf magazine as the 'hardest par-three in the world' which, bearing in mind the 12th at *Augusta National* must have been under consideration, is a remarkable honour to be bestowed by anyone that side of the Atlantic.

The main problem from the tee is the almost non-existent gap there is to aim for through the trees. The cedar tree on the left is the main culprit planted to commemorate the visit of Queen Mary to the castle. Down below is Stockley Beck, which used to supply the course's water but now just collects golf balls in large numbers. The green had to be cut out of the hillside by hand and is not exactly generous, being very narrow and sloping back down the hill.

SHOOT THROUGH THE TREES ON THE 9TH

THE 9TH HAS BEEN NOMINATED THE 'HARDEST PAR-THREE IN THE WORLD'

BRANCEPETH CASTLE – 10TH GREEN

BRANCEPETH CASTLE – TEEING OFF AT THE 10TH

As is usually the case in this situation, having survived the rigours of the 9th, the next hole, the 202-yard par-three 10th, demands a shot back across the same hazard. The only reason it is not considered quite as ferocious as the 9th is because the green is a little more forgiving. *Brancepeth Castle* ends with the 352-yard par-four 18th needing another killer carry across a somewhat more rugged ravine.

Identifying the most difficult hole in Britain that is generally available for the public to play is rather subjective. The par-five 616-yard 3rd at *Orton Meadows*, Cambridgeshire, soon becomes a nomination by many who have attempted it. With water all down its left side, a landing area hidden by trees, with bunkers and thick rough protecting the green, legend has it that the 3rd has never conceded an eagle.

In 2003, whilst playing the 14th at *Orton Meadows*, Vincenzo Frascella was struck by lightning. Recalling the old proverb, and with some fool-hardiness, he continued his round undaunted, until the 17th, when he was struck again.

6

BRIDPORT AND WEST DORSET

BRIDPORT,
DORSET,
DT6 4PS

6TH
PAR 3 - 132 YARDS

PLAYING INTO THE VALLEY ON THE 6TH

Overlooking Lyme Bay, the 6th tee perches 200ft above East Cliff beach. As if the 120ft drop to the fairway is not enough, unkindly, the green is almost totally surrounded by bunkers. If a player draws to the left, his ball simply trickles into another 30ft bunker positioned just short of the cliff face. In winter, the hole plays to a temporary green 20 yards further on. As it is significantly closer to the cliff edge than the usual green, anyone enjoying a bracing stroll on the beach may need to be wary of more than just gull droppings from above.

Inevitably, considering its cliff-top location, the course is often windswept – making the par-fives very hard work. Pick of the long holes is the 15th, blind over a stone wall, playing out of the valley in which the 6th nestles.

For golfers, there can be a small price to pay for enjoying the scenery on cliff-top courses: moulting sea birds like to deposit their feathers on the fairways, so golfers have to search for their ball amongst thousands of 'bogus' white objects.

BRIDPORT AND WEST DORSET – VIEW FROM THE 6TH TEE

Birds present any number of hazards to golfers. Whilst the feathers at *Bridport and West Dorset* can be moved if they interfere with play, a pro, in a qualifying competition for the New Zealand Open, was not so fortunate when sun-baked goose droppings were deemed by the referee to no longer be a loose impediment and so could not be removed, even if he had the stomach for the cleaning up operation.

The town of Bridport attracts many 'grockles' (local slang for tourists, apparently).

Dorset is also the home to a club that has been described as 'the toughest nine-hole course in the country', *Lyons Gate*. Incredibly, no-one has ever managed to play the course to par.

61

BRIGHTON AND HOVE

BRIGHTON,
EAST SUSSEX,
BN1 8YJ

6TH
PAR 3 - 155 YARDS

THE 100FT DROP TO THE 6TH

Though there are plenty of views over the English Channel from *Brighton and Hove*, the course is set back from the sea, four miles north-west of the town centre, near the incredible geological feature of Devil's Dyke, a giant gorge in the South Downs. The 6th is a drop-hole of awesome proportions, a 100ft plunge into the valley below. The picture on the facing page shows that players at the 7th tee are uncomfortably close to the back of the 6th green. They may like to glance up and to the right to prepare for evasive action.

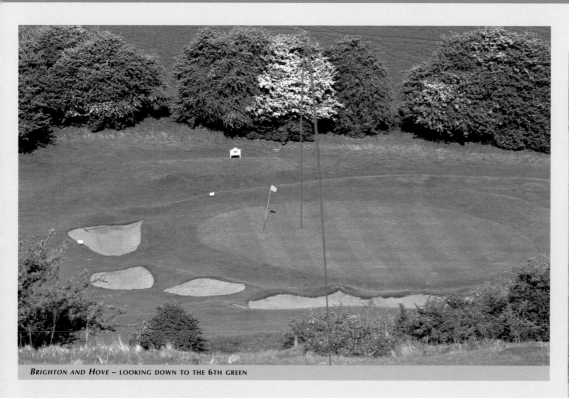

BRIGHTON AND HOVE – LOOKING DOWN TO THE 6TH GREEN

AT 4 YEARS, OVER THE HILL FOR THE YOUNGEST HOLE-IN-ONE

The 6th was the scene of a remarkable hole-in-one achievement. Ray Hoyles, a retired accountant, managed an ace in a friendly game of doubles. Six days later his son, Tim, playing in a competition match did exactly the same – at the same hole.

Golfing folklore is full of hole-in-one oddities, the most freakish in Britain probably being the achievement of a grandmother, Sue Goodwin, who managed two holes-in-one in the same round at *Burnham and Berrow*, Somerset, in 2002. The first, at the 134-yard 5th, was Sue's first ace in 30 years of golf, with the second, like the proverbial London bus, following swiftly at the 140-yard 17th. Even with these heroics, her team still lost the match.

Some golfers like to start early. The world record for the youngest person to get a hole-in-one is held by a five-year-old but a new claim was made in 2001 by three-year-old Jake Paine of California.

Residents of a hamlet near *Brighton and Hove* are rightly fed-up with 'amendments' being made to their signposts.

The correct name of their village is FULKING.

23

BROCKET HALL

WELWYN,
HERTFORDSHIRE,
AL8 7XG

18TH
'BROADWATER'
PAR 5 - 531 YARDS

Set within the grounds of one of England's most imposing stately homes, *Brocket Hall's* two courses are named after the 19th century Prime Ministers who were resident, Lord Melbourne and Lord Palmerston. The Melbourne Course plays back to Brocket Hall in spectacular fashion, with its finishing par-five over the River Lea. It is a fair walk to the nearest bridge so players hop on an electric ferry to get them to the green on the far bank. As with all par-fives playing over water to the green, the trick here is to aim your second shot as close as you dare to the river and leave only a short-iron to reach the other side. There is little room for error as the green is within inches of the far bank. The ferry is out of bounds thus ruining any mad plan of trying to play onto it.

ELECTRIC FERRY TAKES PLAYERS ACROSS TO THE 18TH

Most negotiate the ferry crossing without mishap but players must operate it themselves, leading to the occasional disaster. Operations manager John Wells took a call from a player in distress who had forgotten to turn off his electric trolley whilst standing on the ferry. His bag duly ended up in the river and, although a desperate lunge prevented it from sinking, he could not prevent his keys and 20 balls falling into the drink. The manager spent the afternoon fishing them out. No longer locked out of car and house, the visitor became a member of *Brocket Hall* that day.

Brocket Hall's 395-yard par-four 12th on its Palmerston Course features a 25ft high chalk pit with an almost vertical face. Sitting in the middle of the fairway, 100 yards from the green, it is out of reach for most players from the tee but is an unnerving barrier to approach shots.

Lord Palmerston probably died a happy man. In October 1865, at the age of 80, he is said to have had a fatal heart attack on the billiard table at Brocket Hall in the clutches of a chambermaid.

Today, *Brocket Hall* is one of Britain's leading venues for corporate golf and is home to the first Nick Faldo Golf Institute, a high-tech coaching facility.

BROCKET HALL – CHALK PIT FROM THE 12TH TEE

BROCKET HALL – CHALK PIT ON THE PALMERSTON COURSE 12TH

77

CAMS HALL

FAREHAM,
HAMPSHIRE,
PO16 8UP

**4TH
'THE PRISONER'**
PAR 3 - 209 YARDS

PLAYING INTO THE JAWS OF FAREHAM HARBOUR

CAMS HALL – EASY TO FIND A WATERY GRAVE AT THE 4TH

The club's directions describe the course as being a 'Tiger Woods drive from junction 11 of the M27'. Once at *Cams Hall*, a bit of his golfing ability would not come amiss either on this tricky par-three.

Better known to the public for his commentaries, the BBC's Peter Alliss has also designed many British courses, some, like *Cams Hall*, with a distinct reputation for toughness. Occasionally, during his broadcasts, he puts on his unforgiving golf designer's hat, suggesting recently that the width of the fairways at *Augusta National* is getting rather too generous for the pros.

In fact so difficult was *Cams Hall's* 4th, playing into the jaws of Fareham Harbour, that it was generally treated as a par-four by members until its length was reined back to 209 yards. But even now the creek in front of the green poses a significant challenge and the three bunkers surrounding the green are constantly visited.

In its previous life, at 245 yards, the carry over the water was 230 yards. In a pro-am tournament virtually nobody made it. The hole is an interesting example of a golfing optical illusion. Frequently when there is a lot of 'activity' at the back of a green, players visually underestimate the distance to the pin and, despite what the score card says about the true yardage, tend to underclub. Holes with high trees at the back of a green magnify this effect.

4

CAPE CORNWALL

ST JUST,
CORNWALL,
TR19 7NL

12TH
PAR 4 - 266 YARDS

THE UNCOMFORTABLY NARROW FAIRWAY OF THE 12TH

If you were told that *Cape Cornwall* was one of the country's oldest clubs, you probably wouldn't give the claim a second thought. The 'first and last' course in Britain has the feel of an ancient golfing tract with its walls criss-crossing fairways and Bronze Age settlements. Remarkably though, it was opened in 1990 and is a good example of a modern course that pays homage to golfing history.

The 12th is breathtaking in many ways. It feels as though you are hitting directly into the ocean. The drive plays to a narrow fairway with the land falling away sharply to the right. Inevitably, this area acts as a giant magnet for balls. At the time of our visit, all players seemed helplessly attracted to the hill. Though beautiful in fine weather, Atlantic gales and rain can spell huge trouble for high-handicappers.

Cape Cornwall's par-three 11th, known as the 'Cream Pot', is probably unique for its status as a golf hole enclosed within a walled area. Over its 143 yards there are two marked steps up, leading to a green that nestles within its own mystical sunken garden. The hole stands on the site of a 19th century tin mine. The walls, many of which are half-covered in vegetation, are locally known as 'Cornish hedges'.

Generally the term 'cape' is reserved for an area of land that divides two seas. Cape Cornwall does separate the English and Bristol Channels, though the name may have originated because the area was once thought to be the most westerly point in south-west England, dividing the English Channel from the Atlantic Ocean. But along came the Ordnance Survey who demonstrated that it was in fact Land's End that could stake that claim. Countering the image of the Atlantic as a vast grey swell, the sea around Cape Cornwall is actually an almost Mediterranean deep blue.

CAPE CORNWALL – MULTI-STEPPED PAR-THREE 11TH

A MODERN COURSE THAT PAYS HOMAGE TO GOLFING HISTORY

CAPE CORNWALL – 'SECRET GARDEN' 11TH GREEN

CARNOUSTIE

ANGUS,
DD7 7JE

17TH
PAR 4 - 433 YARDS

BARRY BURN SNAKES ITS WAY BACK AND FORTH OVER THE 17TH FAIRWAY

The longest and, in most players' judgement, the toughest Championship course in Britain, *Carnoustie*, has had a mixed relationship with the golfing powers. Dropped from the Open rota for almost 50 years, it struck back by providing the most difficult layout in the history of the competition when in 1999 the rough was so thick that the tour pros were left thrashing around and fuming.

Barry Burn has to be played over seven times during an average round, twice on the 17th. Here the burn winds its way through the fairway in an 'S' shaped coil.

Drifting to the left from the tee is virtually guaranteed to find the water and anything going right, some of the most dense and unforgiving rough on the planet. The burn has to be crossed a second time for the wood or long-iron approach shot to a green with a pronounced right-to-left slope that is peppered with bunkers.

The 17th takes its place within what is considered to be the hardest four-hole finishing stretch on any of the Championship courses. At 245 yards, the 16th is at the limits of par-three status. The 18th was the scene of Jean Van de Velde's heart-rending eight when he threw away the British Open in 1999, famously taking a paddle in Barry Burn with the certifiable idea of attempting to play his ball out.

THE ROUGH WAS SO THICK, THE PROS WERE LEFT THRASHING AROUND AND FUMING

TEIGN VALLEY – THE DIRECT ROUTE OVER THE DOGLEG FOR A HOLE-IN-ONE ON THE 17TH

Away from the glare of the cameras, amateurs occasionally make golfing history.

Golfing records are rarely as straightforward as they should be, and this includes the accolade of the 'longest hole-in-one' achieved on a British course. There is a subtle difference between the longest hole that has been aced and the longest shot to achieve an ace. It is the existence of dogleg holes that complicates the picture. The 17th at *Teign Valley*, Devon, 'The Manor', measures 496 yards, 93 yards longer than anyone has ever managed to drive a golf ball. But in 1995, bypassing the fairway route completely and instead launching one over the trees to the left, Shaun Lynch managed the incredible feat of striking his first shot straight into the hole. This achievement is recognised by the Guinness Book of Records, which lists the 'longest hole-in-one' (i.e. the longest actual carry) separately. This is credited to Brian Connolly who aced the 374-yard par-four 18th at *Fereneze*, East Renfrewshire.

SIGN AT *TEIGN VALLEY'S* 17TH

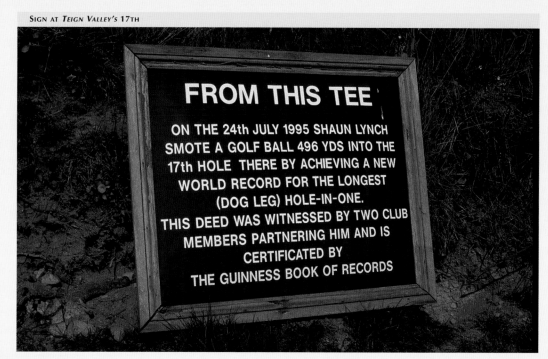

FROM THIS TEE
ON THE 24th JULY 1995 SHAUN LYNCH
SMOTE A GOLF BALL 496 YDS INTO THE
17th HOLE THERE BY ACHIEVING A NEW
WORLD RECORD FOR THE LONGEST
(DOG LEG) HOLE-IN-ONE.
THIS DEED WAS WITNESSED BY TWO CLUB
MEMBERS PARTNERING HIM AND IS
CERTIFICATED BY
THE GUINNESS BOOK OF RECORDS

99

CARRADALE

KINTYRE,
ARGYLL AND BUTE,
PA28 6QT

6TH
'PUDDING BOWL'
PAR 4 - 320 YARDS

LOB ONTO THE ARMCHAIR GREEN

On the west coast of Kintyre, the internationally renowned *Machrihanish* uses its sea aspect to great effect. On the east are the lesser known nine holes of *Carradale*, a tight moorland course with views across the bay to Arran that rival any from a British course.

None of the greens are particularly large and the positioning of the 6th is very unusual. The rolling fairway does not exactly extend seamlessly to the putting area. Instead the green is offset up a sharp bank to the right, needing an accurate lob over rocks. It is formed into an almost perfect armchair shape, built up on three sides with generously cut slopes that can take a ball to the heart of the green if you manage to pitch your ball onto one of the banks.

CARRADALE – AVOID THE OUT OF BOUNDS BEACH

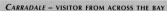

CARRADALE – VISITOR FROM ACROSS THE BAY

Carradale offers a spectacular par-three 7th, 'Port Righ' (240 yards), with the beach out of bounds to the left and gardens on the right, and an intimidating carry over rough.

All the greens can be enclosed within electric fences as the course has some distinctive four-legged visitors. *Carradale* is popular with wild goats that cross the bay at low tide to enquire if golfers have any spare sandwiches or, if disappointed, simply go and chomp away at plants in local gardens. Though inquisitive, they are unlikely to surprise players from behind, as you can usually smell them before you see them. They are said to have come over with the Spanish Armada but, after hundreds of years, they still have not got used to Kintyre's environment, and are often seen looking forlorn on top of rocks in the bay, having become stranded by the incoming tide.

79

CHART HILLS

BIDDENDEN,
KENT,
TN27 8JX

16TH
PAR 5 - 506 YARDS

As far as we know, the nearest thing to a collective noun for bunkers is 'nest'. But the term does not really do justice to the scene from the 16th tee at *Chart Hills* where, stretching out into the distance, there appears to be more sand than grass. Over its 506 yards there are 19 bunkers, 15 of which form an almost continuous line to the right of the fairway on your second shot. Assuming the fairway is safely reached from the tee, the next shot plays to the left over the four bunkers in the foreground and uphill onto a fairway that progressively narrows on its way to the green.

THE BUNKER INFESTED PAR-FIVE 16TH

Chart Hills is the brainchild of six times major winner, Nick Faldo. It was the first European course he designed and is characterised by a multitude of water hazards and at least 140 immaculate white sand bunkers. The 200 metre 'Anaconda' bunker, that stretches along and across the 5th fairway, is the longest in Britain.

Faldo opened the course in 1993 by hitting a drive 285 yards down the middle of the 1st fairway. When challenged to put another ball 'next to the first one', he played an identical shot landing within 18 inches of the first ball. They have not moved since, having been set into wood at the spot where they landed.

CHART HILLS – NICK FALDO'S OPENING DAY DRIVES

Chart Hills' 17th is a 147-yard par-three played entirely over water to an island green. The cottage across the road should be safe from stray shots. Recently, the owner was surprised to be asked 'can I have my putter back?' by a player who had lost his cool and flung the club into the garden.

CHART HILLS – ANOTHER CLUTCH OF BUNKERS TO CONQUER AT THE 9TH

CHART HILLS – 17TH OVER WATER

CHILTERN FOREST

AYLESBURY,
BUCKINGHAMSHIRE,
HP22 5NQ

8TH
'THE BADGER'
PAR 3 - 160 YARDS

Underclubbing is a constant problem for amateur golfers, made worse when the flag perches on top of a hill. The flag on the 8th at *Chiltern Forest* is rarely reached by visitors from the tee: it requires a wood, or at the very least a sturdy five-iron, but invariably most fall short. Its difficulty is such that most treat losing a shot to par as a good score.

Estimates of the height of the hill vary wildly – ranging from 80 to 200ft. The truth probably lies somewhere in the middle. The 8th (and the 2nd) play straight over the 12th fairway at the foot of the hill. A path darts its way to the top diagonally up the slope. At the summit players are faced with a tiny green that has been moulded into an almost perfect square shape.

OVER THE 12TH FAIRWAY UP TO THE 8TH GREEN

CHILTERN FOREST – THE 8TH PLAYS LONGER THAN IT LOOKS

Chiltern Forest's present-day layout is far from standard, requiring a number of rules about which players have priority where holes collide. Unusually, the first three holes cut diagonally across the hilly split-level course.

St Andrews Old Course, Fife, features a number of criss-crossing fairways, but the best example of holes colliding is perhaps at *Verulam*, Hertfordshire, where the 4th and 9th holes cross at 90 degrees. Strict 'right of way' rules apply which members enjoy pointing out to confused visitors.

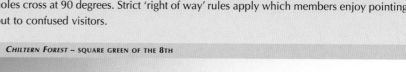

CHILTERN FOREST – SQUARE GREEN OF THE 8TH

Although golf has been played on the site for around 100 years, a proper club was not established until 1992 following the purchase of land from the Ministry of Defence and Forestry Commission. The original six-hole course included a mammoth par-six playing from the site of the new clubhouse to the current-day first green.

70

CLAYTON

BRADFORD,
WEST YORKSHIRE,
BD14 6JX

8TH 'SPION KOP'

PAR 4 - 287 YARDS

THE CLIMB TO THE PEAK OF 'SPION KOP'

The area to the west of Bradford City Centre is best known for its 'curry mile' along Great Horton Road as it makes its way up to the highest village in England, Queensbury. There is a sharp drop to the village of Clayton below. Perched on the side of the hill is probably the steepest upward hole in England.

Clayton's nine holes have recently been rearranged and extended to provide two par-fives. Its 8th (formerly the 7th) requires an approach shot up a slope so steep that steps have been built to help players make it to the green.

CLAYTON – LOOKING BACK TO THE 8TH TEE

The shot is complicated by the fact that the highest point on the course is ravaged by strong winds for much of the year. At the time of our visit, the flag position was unfeasibly close to the edge of the precipice. The hole can be negotiated with a good drive and a wedge up the hill – but it is prone to produce the ultimate golfer's nightmare: a well–hit shot that manages to roll back, finishing behind him.

CLAYTON – TWO SHOTS TO CONQUER THE GREEN ON THE 8TH

The term 'Spion Kop' is generally associated with football, particularly the home stand at Liverpool Football Club. Its name derives from a hill in South Africa which saw a bloody battle between British and Boers in 1900. The British killed there mostly came from Liverpool and Lancashire regiments, hence the connection with the football club.

West Yorkshire's other feared uphill slog is at Gotts Park in the heavily urban area of Armley, Leeds. The course features four opening holes playing in and out of the valley of the River Aire, the most physically testing being the 5th, a par-four, where, for the approach shot to the green, players face a 140-yard scramble up a bank, provoking moans from all but the super-fit.

COLLINGTREE PARK

NORTHAMPTON,
NORTHAMPTONSHIRE,
NN4 0XN

18TH

PAR 5 - 543 YARDS

Whilst North American courses do not feature the more romantic, rugged aspects of British layouts, they are full of superb artificial features such as greens balanced on water-surrounded islands; the world famous 17th at *Sawgrass* being a perfect case in point. There are surprisingly few 'true' island greens in the UK. Perhaps the most perfect example is just off junction 15 of the M1 at *Collingtree Park*, twice host of the British Masters.

There is water all the way down the right of the not particularly generous fairway. The second shot must lay up as close as possible to the end of a narrow peninsula, so avoiding an early dip into the water. There is a 50-yard carry from the tip of the peninsula to the flag, as the lake sweeps around from the left to form a lagoon in which the green is stranded. A narrow wooden bridge takes players from behind the putting area over the water to a less than forgiving putting surface, with everything sloping back towards the fairway.

ACROSS WATER TO THE 18TH GREEN

COLLINGTREE PARK – A RARE ISLAND GREEN AT THE 18TH

BRANSTON – A RATHER PUBLIC FINISHER OVER THE LILY POND

If you have the misfortune of finding the water at *Collingtree Park*, at least you do not have an audience. But at *Branston Golf and Country Club*, Staffordshire, players have to negotiate an approach over a pond at the 18th, 'Lily Pit' (325 yards), in front of a gallery of diners on the veranda of the clubhouse. Taking bets on which players will make it provides an amusing lunchtime diversion. Olympic gold medallist oarsman Matthew Pinsent recalls his experience at the 18th as amongst his worst sporting moments when, in his own words, he "choked down on a wedge and flopped the ball straight into the middle of the lake – I wish I could have followed it in."

43

CRONDON PARK

STOCK,
ESSEX,
CM4 9DP

18TH 'CRONDON CRUNCH'
PAR 5/6 - 860 YARDS

APPROACH SHOT ON THE MAMMOTH 18TH

A number of entries in The Guinness Book of Records are hotly debated. For instance, there are many claimants to the title of Britain's oldest pub. The accolade of Britain's longest golf hole is, surprisingly, not as clear-cut as it could be. For decades, Britain's longest hole has been recognised as the 2nd par-five at *Gedney Hill*, Lincolnshire, at 671 yards. At the time of writing, *Crondon Park's* club card lists the yardage of its 18th at 655 from the back tee, leaving it as the longest finishing hole in Britain, but some way behind *Gedney Hill* for the ultimate honour. However, the club has constructed another tee 200 yards further back that, technically, brings the yardage to a jaw-dropping 860. At this distance, unless you are hitting straight as an arrow, it means a walk of over half a mile just to complete one hole. That should be game, set and match to *Crondon Park*. However, the tee is only used for exhibition matches and fun competitions, meaning that visitors currently will not get a crack at the monster. When the hole is ratified by the Golfing Union as a par-six, members and visitors will get the chance to play from the back tee.

Then things get more complicated. Enter, stage left, *Dewstow*, Monmouth-shire, whose recently extended 13th 'Forestry' weighs in at 700 yards, making it Britain's only existing par-six. As this is routinely available for members and visitors to play, purists might argue that, for a short while, *Dewstow's* 13th takes the honour.

Nevertheless, *Crondon Park's* finisher provides the perfect setting for long driving contests. In 2001, World Champion Carl Woodward, made the green in two from the back tee. In 1997, he achieved the longest drive ever recorded, in Tenerife, an unlikely sounding 408 yards and 10 inches, easily in excess of anything achievable by the game's acknowledged long-hitters, including Tiger Woods.

The World's longest hole is the 964-yard par-seven 3rd at *Satsuki Golf Club*, Japan. Conveniently skirting the issue, recent editions of The Guiness Book of Records have no entry for the longest hole in Britain.

CRONDON PARK – 4TH TO WATER-PROTECTED GREEN

There are many other highlights at *Crondon Park* before tackling the enormous 18th. The 4th features a classic island green. The 159-yard 7th plays almost entirely over water.

CRONDON PARK – 14TH; ITS VERSION OF THE FAMOUS 12TH AT AUGUSTA NATIONAL, USA

CRONDON PARK – 7TH PLAYED ALMOST ENTIRELY OVER WATER

68

CRUDEN BAY

PETERHEAD,
ABERDEENSHIRE,
AB42 0NN

14TH 'WHINS'
PAR 4 - 397 YARDS

SUNKEN GREEN AT THE 14TH WITH THE 15TH TEE ON THE RIGHT

No matter how prestigious a top British course is, there are always some moans from the terminally picky golfer. In fact it has become voguish to knock the Old Course at *St Andrews*. But everyone who sets eyes on *Cruden Bay* has nothing but superlatives for these links set amongst strange, tumbling dunes.

Playing in and out of the stumpy hills means tackling many blind shots. Having negotiated the drive from the 14th tee, in which the North Sea to the right acts as a lateral water hazard, the second shot is completely blind to one of the more incredible greens in the land. The 14th putting area is hidden away in a deep punchbowl with steep slopes on three sides and steps leading down to the right.

The photograph on the facing page also shows the heart-stopping blind tee shot of the next hole, the 239-yard par-three 15th 'Blin' Dunt', with its tee to the right and above the 14th green. The perfect line for the shot is straight over the hill on the left-hand side.

THE SHOT TO THE NATURAL BOWL OF *CRUDEN BAY'S* 14TH GREEN

It is possible that golf has been played on this land since 1791, and although the course was largely redeveloped in 1926, some of the original layout is still in evidence. *Cruden Bay* has views over to the unsettling, abandoned 'Slains Castle', inspiration for Bram Stoker's 'Dracula'.

Scotland's generally accepted claim as the home of golf was not questioned until a German sports historian, Heiner Gillmeister, claimed in 2002 that the first visual evidence of the game was in a Dutch painting of a man appearing to hit a small ball with a stick. He dismissed the earlier 15th century Scottish evidence as a type of 'street hockey'.

CULLEN

MORAY,
AB56 4WB

12TH 'NEAVES'
PAR 3 - 182 YARDS

*C*ullen must lay claim to the most remarkable site for a golf course in Europe. Packed into a narrow strip of land between the sea and a sheer cliff face, its 18 holes dart in and out of a series of huge clumps of dusty red rock, providing all manner of gullies, ravines and plateaus. The largest and most imposing of these, Boarcrag, sits in the centre of the course and has to be avoided on the 12th.

PLAYING AROUND AND OVER *CULLEN'S* STALKS OF ROCK

CULLEN – A SCARY APPROACH TO THE 13TH GREEN

CULLEN – BOARCRAG DOMINATES THE HEART OF THE COURSE

There is not a lot of room within this amazing environment for *Cullen's* 18 holes, with the course playing its outward nine close to the cliff before doing an about-turn with the inward nine playing back at beach level. At 4597 yards long, it does manage to fit in a 510-yard par-five 15th.

The one key variation to its circular layout is at the 12th which plays directly across the 11th green. The par-three heads back inland requiring you to dodge Boarcrag on the left and carry another vast rocky outcrop just before the green.

The largest trio of *Cullen's* stalks of rock are called the 'Three Kings'. At the blind par-three 13th a clump is directly in the line of fire, requiring a shot straight over the top of a sandstone mound. Helpfully, there is a red arrow painted on the side facing the tee showing the best line to the green.

44

DAINTON PARK

IPPLEPEN,
DEVON,
TQ12 5TN

8TH
PAR 3 - 183 YARDS

THE SAND-ENCLOSED 8TH GREEN

ESCAPE FROM THE CIRCULAR BUNKER

At the highest point of this modern parkland course there is a gazebo housing a drinks machine for those in need of sustenance before taking on the 8th.

There is a 50ft drop down to a remarkable example of an island green, encircled not by water but one vast bunker varying in width between 8 and 20ft. In places the bunker is

four feet deep. The only access to the green is by two narrow footbridges. Many simply opt to play short from the tee and try to get away with a bogey-four.

The nearby railway town of Newton Abbot provided the sleepers that adorn many features of the course. The bunker at the 8th is built up with them and they have also been used to good effect in the construction of layered tee areas. *Dainton Park* also has a fairly unusual driving range, playing up a steep hill.

DAINTON PARK – SLEEPERED TEE AREA

Another frightening bunker protects the front of the green at the 311-yard par-four 4th at *Sandhill*, South Yorkshire. The very deep pot-bunker has sand moulded into a series of steps with the green forming a horseshoe shape around it.

AN UNUSUAL BUNKER PROTECTS THE FRONT OF THE GREEN AT SANDHILL

SANDHILL – STEPPED POT-BUNKER ON THE 4TH

9

DARTMOUTH

BLACKAWTON,
DEVON,
TQ9 7DE

18TH
PAR 3 - 179 YARDS

DARTMOUTH'S CLASSIC FINISHER

Of all our 100 extraordinary holes, the 18th at *Dartmouth* is probably the most accessible. You don't even need to get out of the car to view golfers taking on this amazing closing hole. From the stylish country club building (which packs in a pool and gym), many of the flags of the nine and eighteen-hole courses can be seen dotted around the steep hill to the north. The 18th green sits in the valley. To find the teeing areas, you have to look across the generous buggy path, over a substantial lake, and up a vertical height of around 50ft. Clearing the lake (often playing into the wind) can be a major struggle for the average player.

DARTMOUTH – 3RD OVER A LAKE TO THE SLOPING GREEN

The 18th might feel less testing if it came at the end of a middling course. But *Dartmouth's* Championship layout contains a number of classic holes, making the finisher the mere icing on the cake. Renowned for its superbly maintained (though far from flat) greens, it has 12 water features in addition to the streams that wind their way through the course.

The par-three 3rd on the Championship Course is a classic drop-hole over water to a sloping green. The 10th features one of the most forbidding tee shots and unforgiving fairways in the country. Teeing off from a raised position at the side of the clubhouse, the drive plays down to a fairway running at 30 degrees across the line of fire. Even a good tee shot that gets an unkind bounce can easily drift out of bounds.

DARTMOUTH – NOT A LOT TO AIM FOR AT THE 10TH

DEWSBURY DISTRICT

MIRFIELD,
WEST YORKSHIRE,
WF14 8HJ

17TH 'BUTTS'
PAR 4 - 402 YARDS

Many clubs can claim that their layout has remained essentially the same since formation, but *Dewsbury District* has had so many mini-redesigns that visiting golfers can expect a few new adjustments each season. Its current layout has one of the most daunting parkland carries we have found. From the high medal tee, it requires a drive of 200 yards to carry a copse to the fairway in the valley below. The timid can attempt to skirt round to the right, but with mature trees everywhere, you might as well go for glory.

200 YARDS OVER THE COPSE FROM THE MEDAL TEE

Though you will have little idea of its fate, your ball should scuttle down the slope the other side leaving a short-iron to the green that is protected by a pond and contains an unusual step down across a wall.

One feature of *Dewsbury District* that has remained unchanged for most of the club's history is the troublesome lumps and bumps of the 9th green, a 132-yard par-three. An odd facet of the layout is the out of bounds that sweep through the heart of the course, including an area very close to the 9th green and another unexpected boundary splitting the 10th. Newcomers are sometimes perturbed by how good shots, seemingly on-target, find their way into internal out of bounds.

DEWSBURY DISTRICT – THE RUN DOWN THE HILL TO THE 17TH GREEN

DEWSBURY DISTRICT – 9TH WITH ITS SLOPES AND BORROWS

Unusually for a full-length eighteen-hole course, *Dewsbury District* ends with a par-three. It gets topped by the seaside links at *Reay*, Highland, which, at 5831 yards, manages to start and finish with a par-three.

THE TROUBLESOME LUMPS AND BUMPS OF THE 9TH GREEN

DEWSTOW

CAERWENT,
MONMOUTHSHIRE,
NP26 5AH

13TH
'FORESTRY'
PAR 6 - 700 YARDS

BRITAIN'S ONLY PAR-SIX

PLAYERS SHOULD NOT HAVE TAKEN MORE THAN 2 HOURS							
10		Two Tees	191	116	3	15	
11		Little Park	378	342	4	5	
12		Ekki Bridge	134	130	3	17	
13		Forestry	585 700	570 695	5 6	3	
14		Keeper's Lodge	466	448	4	1	
15		Totem	414	403	4	7	

I n trying to entangle the debate about Britain's longest hole, there are two things that can be stated with reasonable certainty. At the time of publication, *Dewstow's* colossal 13th is the longest that a casual golfer can actually play on, that is until *Crondon Park* opens its 860-yard tee on the 18th to the public. It is also the only official par-six in the UK.

With the aid of a zoom lens at full tilt, it is just possible to make out the flag to the right of the hump in the middle of the picture – though necessarily the space between tee and green is considerably foreshortened here. In reality, it can take a good drive and two more hefty fairway woods to even get a sniff at the green. Playing the hole as a par-six is 'optional'.

THE 13TH CAN BE PLAYED AS A PAR-FIVE OR PAR-SIX

You could play the 2nd at *Braemar*, Aberdeenshire, 10 times before you would have covered the distance of *Dewstow's* 13th. *Braemar's* idyllic signature hole, measuring just 69 yards, is a feature of the highest eighteen-hole course in the UK.

DEWSTOW'S SECRET GARDEN

DEWSTOW – TOTEM POLE IN MIDDLE OF THE 15TH

Recently a series of secret gardens and grottoes were discovered on the site near the course. Much of the garden's layout has been buried for 60 years and has undergone major restoration in readiness for opening to the public in 2003.

Dewstow opened in 1988 and has been a commercial success story, whereas other clubs in rural areas have often struggled. Part of the secret has been very low membership fees, helping *Dewstow* achieve the highest membership in Wales.

GOLFING THEMES ON TOTEM POLE

Just as you have recovered from the long excursion up the 13th, a remarkable man-made feature appears on *Dewstow's* 15th – a 50ft high totem pole. It was hand-carved by a local sculptor, in-situ, out of an ailing American redwood tree. Every symbol relates to golf or the surrounding area, including the three 'golfing birds', an albatross, an eagle and a 'birdie'. The totem pole is very much in-play, standing in the middle of the fairway.

27

DUFFTOWN

KEITH,
MORAY,
AB55 4BS

10TH
'GLENFIDDICH'
PAR 4 - 462 YARDS

A little effort is needed to make it to the turn for home but, at the peak of *Dufftown*, set in the heart of whisky country, players are rewarded with arguably the most stunning inland tee shot in the country. Golfers love the chance to open the shoulders and launch a drive into a generous valley, though in this case an avenue of conifers has to be negotiated before the relative safety of the expanse of fairway. The green, a mere dot in the distance, lies 339ft below, almost certainly the biggest tee-to-green drop in Britain. The tee perches 1213ft above sea level, just beaten by the course's 9th tee at 1294ft, the highest in Scotland. Only *Braemar*, Aberdeenshire, 30 miles south of *Dufftown*, can compete for such lofty holes.

THE BIGGEST TEE-TO-GREEN DROP IN BRITAIN

339FT DROP TO 10TH GREEN

DUFFTOWN – THE 7TH IS BRITAIN'S JOINT SHORTEST HOLE

DUFFTOWN – LOOKING BACK UP TO THE 10TH TEE

Dufftown and *Braemar* are very close in their claim for the highest land for a British golf course, and they share the honour of having the country's shortest 'proper' hole. *Dufftown's* 7th, 'Fittie Burn', plays across a deep gully, though at only 67 yards it is not exactly a test of brute force. Spreading the net wider than established golf courses, the shortest pitch-and-putt hole in the country is probably the 1st at *Bruntwood Park*, Cheadle Hulme, Cheshire, where, depending on the pin position, it weighs in at around 25 yards long.

Students from Aberdeen University attempted to set a sort of British altitude sporting record: hitting golf balls up the face of Ben Nevis. Having lost 256 balls, they honourably gave up.

IN THE CLOUDS AT DUFFTOWN'S 9TH

DUKES MEADOWS

CHISWICK,
LONDON,
W4 2SH

8TH
PAR 3 - 138 YARDS

The hallowed turf of *St Andrews* must be the most sacred in golf but, from a financial rather than historical point of view, *Dukes Meadows* is probably the most valuable course per square foot. Occupying a prime site in desirable West London, tucked into land at the bend of the River Thames just to the west of Chiswick Bridge, *Dukes Meadows* is designed for executive golf; a relatively quick nine holes in the afternoon after work or, if the boss is not looking, during lunch.

PROBABLY THE MOST VALUABLE COURSE PER SQUARE FOOT

THE FOUR TIERS OF THE 8TH GREEN

Clearly, due to its central location, you are not going to get any raking par-fives here but, what *Dukes Meadows* lacks in length (its nine holes total just 1105 yards), it makes up for with a host of ingeniously placed water features and some amazing greens.

The 8th is our pick, since it has the possibly unique claim of containing four separate tiers. Also watch out for the hump in the middle of the 3rd, the unusual 'U' shaped 2nd and the 6th with a hollow in the middle.

THE PICCADILLY LINE RUNNING THROUGH *WYKE GREEN*

Add in the nearby aggregate business with the railway shunting yard and *Wyke Green* is probably the noisiest course in Britain but, it is in great condition and being quite flat, makes for very pleasant golf for the few people who actually remain in London at the weekend.

THE 11TH AT *WYKE GREEN* RUNS PARALLEL TO THE M4

Aside from *Dukes Meadows*, Central London is a bit of a golfing wilderness. However, if you have no time to escape to the leafy suburbs, the capital does have a few oases but you cannot expect a tranquil hush to descend during your round. *Wyke Green* in Isleworth, West London, lies at the epicentre of London's chaotic transport infrastructure, below the flight path to Heathrow (which is just four miles away), with a motorway on one boundary and the Piccadilly Underground line (in an overground section) running straight through the middle. In fact, a slice from the 18th can easily find its way onto the line and at the 11th tee, it is possible to put one on the west carriageway of the M4.

14

DURNESS

BALNAKEIL,
HIGHLAND,
IV27 4PG

9TH
PAR 3 - 108 YARDS

Durness can claim to be the only British mainland course where it is possible to complete a round after normal pub closing time. As the most northerly course on the British mainland, in summer darkness does not descend until the early hours of the morning allowing it to have a competition with midnight tee-off times. But anyone considering taking on the short 5545-yard course after a few drinks needs to be aware of *Durness'* main feature – the most precipitous tee in Britain.

The 9th teeing area lies just two feet short of a sheer 60ft drop to the crashing waves below. If the vertigo doesn't unsettle you, the shot itself could bring on a touch of queasiness – a 100-yard carry across the Atlantic Ocean. A very rough path leads down to the sea, though those crazy enough to clamber down to look for a ball report that the risk is not worth taking.

BRITAIN'S MOST PRECIPITOUS TEE

THE SEA CARRY AT THE 9TH

GORLESTON – THE 8TH TEE IS THREATENING TO FALL INTO THE NORTH SEA DUE TO EROSION

PRIVATE LAND
THIS IS NOT A PUBLIC FOOTPATH
WARNING
YOU ARE IN DANGER OF BEING FATALLY INJURED BY FLYING GOLF BALLS
Also PARTS OF THE CLIFF EDGE ARE UNSTABLE AND ARE LIABLE TO COLLAPSE

DIRE WARNINGS FOR CLIFF-TOP WALKERS AT GORLESTON

Although there is no dispute over *Durness'* status as the most northerly mainland course, and Cornwall's *Mullion* and *Cape Cornwall* are easily identified as the most southerly and westerly, it takes very close examination of a map to discover the most easterly. *Great Yarmouth and Caister* vies with *Gorleston* for the privilege, within five miles of each other on the Norfolk coast.

The answer, for geographical anoraks, is that the most easterly point at which it is possible to play a legal golf shot is from the 8th tee at *Gorleston*, though conceivably, someone playing the 7th (in the background of our picture) could leave their ball precariously on the cliff edge. In the 1980s, the 7th was rescued from the ravages of the North Sea – coastal erosion being a constant headache on the east coast.

EREWASH VALLEY

STANTON-BY-DALE,
DERBYSHIRE,
DE7 4QR

4TH 'QUARRY'
PAR 3 - 92 YARDS

Considering Derbyshire has some of England's grandest scenery, golf courses are quite thin on the ground. *Erewash Valley* has many holes playing parallel to each other but, when it breaks out of a standard format, it does so in spectacular fashion. The 4th and 5th nestle on their own in a heavily wooded Victorian quarry. Visitors should note that the quarry holes are not playable in winter.

The charming tiny par-three 4th plays into the heart of the quarry with its green placed tight against the rock face. A wedge should be sufficient, with anything a touch long pitching directly into the quarry wall with unpredictable results.

Once down in the base of *Erewash Valley's* quarry, there is the par-three 5th (147 yards) to tackle before the clamber out. Playing under the line of the 4th, it can require some draw to successfully make the green in one.

CAREFUL OF THE QUARRY FACE AT THE 4TH

EREWASH VALLEY – THE 5TH GREEN WITH THE 4TH PLAYING OVERHEAD

The name of the 5th, 'In the Quarry', is about as direct and descriptive as you could wish for. But British hole names are generally a bizarre bunch at the best of times, conjuring up all sorts of unlikely images, the most unholy of which are to be found at the otherwise tranquil *Mannings Heath*, West Sussex where the 2nd and 3rd are called 'Sodom' and 'Gomorrah'.

Otherwise these are a selection of the oddest we have come across on our travels:

Llandrindod Wells 10th	–	'KITCHEN'
Stonehaven 10th	–	'SLUGHEAD'
Stonehaven 16th	–	'RASHES'
Strathendrick 2nd	–	'BEANIES DINK'
Lochcarron 4th	–	'THE DOCTOR'
Lochcarron 5th	–	'FLYING ANT'
Cams Hall 24th	–	'SCHOOL DOG'
Charnwood Forest 16th	–	'GRUNTERS'

1

EYEMOUTH

BORDERS,
TD14 5SF

6TH
'A-STILL-NO-KEN'
PAR 3 - 170 YARDS

THE TEE SHOT OVER THE ABYSS

THE CLUB'S PRO CUES UP FOR *EYEMOUTH'S* 6TH ... YES, HE DID MAKE IT

... AND THE PHOTOGRAPHER DIDN'T

It is probably a blessing that visitors to *Eyemouth*, the most southerly Scottish course, may be blissfully unaware of what is about to hit them. The clubhouse is set well back from the North Sea coast with a road separating the first four holes from the bulk of the course that plays along the cliffs. There is a comparatively easy-going warm-up with a shot over Puddocks Pond on the par-three 3rd. But nothing can prepare you for the assault upon your senses when turning the corner for the 6th tee. Britain's most extraordinary golf hole plays over a magnificent rocky inlet, with the sea churning below. It is definitely not recommended for those with a fear of heights.

There are three tee locations on the north side of the chasm with the outermost whites playing to 170 yards – though looking over the void, it can seem closer to double that distance. The jagged points of rock rising from the ocean give the sense of being transported back into prehistory. The only respite is that there is a reasonably generous landing area the other side, with some room for error. The inlet is classed as a water hazard, so there is a dropping area to go to after the inevitable mishaps. The course planner helpfully advises to "take plenty of club here or it's another freebie for King Neptune".

UPHILL TO THE 7TH GREEN

At the southern tip of Loch Ness, *Fort Augustus* is bordered by the Glengarry Mountains, which even in summer can retain snow on their peaks. Despite its natural rugged feel, its construction (in 1927) was an immense project involving widespread tree clearance on unforgiving rocky ground.

Fort Augustus has a reputation as Scotland's most challenging nine-hole course. The 7th is a 'borderline' par-three, playing uphill all the way, with a 3ft fence to negotiate before the green. The nine holes each have different teeing positions to complete an

FORT AUGUSTUS – THE FENCE ON THE 7TH FAIRWAY

FORT AUGUSTUS – SHEEP ROAM FREELY ON THE HIGHLAND COURSE

eighteen-hole round. For the second nine, the 7th becomes the 16th. Playing from just 20 yards further back, it now gains par-four status.

The layout has a distinctive browny yellow tinge with acres of heather and gorse lining the fairways. The heather is a particularly tightly knit variety meaning that a ball caught up in it is only just retrievable, with a short recovery shot back onto the fairway being the only realistic option.

Sheep roam lazily around the whole course, ambling out of the way of golfers when necessary. Ex-club secretary John Morgan reports that he played a shot off-target that managed to hit a sheep on its horn, ricocheting the ball onto the green.

FULFORD HEATH

WYTHALL,
WORCESTERSHIRE,
B47 6BH

16TH
PAR 3 - 166 YARDS

Though playing over water is not particularly unusual, negotiating a large pond to a green that is on a raised area is uniquely testing. One particular member, who can remain anonymous, managed to hit 12 successive tee shots into the pond. Locals have informally named the hole after him.

OVER THE POND...AND UP

Many holes play far longer than they look, inevitably leading to underclubbing. But the difficulty with *Fulford Heath's* 16th is the other way round – it looks somewhat longer than its 140-yard carry. The effect of this is to intimidate the player from the tee so much that he turns to jelly just at the moment that a cool head is required. The green itself is a difficult, rolling affair, protected by three bunkers.

British golf clubs are often meticulous in their recording of committee minutes. *Fulford Heath* provides a particularly baffling entry for 10th March 1935: "The Secretary to see Nadim: re jumping cow". The club's millennium book features a refreshingly large number of drinking stories, including a contest between members to test the effects of whisky versus beer on golfing performance. Having either a large scotch or pint of beer on every hole, the contest finished with an inevitably messy conclusion on the 6th. History does not record which side won, though they were all probably past caring.

Another classic par-three over water is the 5th 'Oasis' (208 yards) at *The Oxfordshire*. The red, yellow and white teeing areas are slightly more generously positioned on both the left and right-hand side of the lake, but from the back tee players have to contend with the full carry over the water with no less than 10 bunkers dotted around to the left of the green.

THE OXFORDSHIRE – THE FULL CARRY OVER WATER AT THE 5TH

GALASHIELS

**BORDERS,
TD1 2NJ**

10TH 'THE HILL'
PAR 4 - 272 YARDS

LOOKING BACK TO THE TOWN FROM THE 10TH GREEN

THE CLIMB UP THE 10TH HAS MANY GASPING

The Secretary at *Galashiels* reports that it has been known for arriving players to pull up at the club, take one look at the challenge ahead and turn the vehicle around in a hurry. The feature that gives them this sudden change of heart is the punishing hill, one-in-three in places, that dominates the early holes. The only flat ground you will find is on the teeing areas and greens. But those feeling too fragile to take on the course are missing the glorious finishing holes that wind their way back towards the clubhouse. The 10th has a generously wide fairway, but is a relentless climb to the top with out of bounds all the way up the right-hand side. The green itself has been built up at the front end to give a rare flat surface.

The highest point at *Galashiels* is 1100ft above sea level, a significant climb in itself, without having the encumbrance of a set of golf clubs. The name of the 11th, 'Nearly There', provides a clue that there is respite soon. There is the extra challenge of a wall running across the fairway on the 12th. A sigh of relief is finally deserved at the 13th 'The Summit', where the efforts are rewarded with stunning views over the Borders' countryside.

> ## THE ONLY FLAT GROUND YOU WILL FIND IS ON THE TEEING AREAS AND GREENS

GREAT VIEWS ONCE YOU HAVE SCALED THE HEIGHTS OF *GALASHIELS*

GALASHIELS – WALL ACROSS THE 12TH FAIRWAY

The visitors' book at the course gives a flavour of how tough golfers find it:

"Doctor with oxygen required at 11th"
"Remember to bring another set of knees"
"9th and 10th good practice for the Himalayan Open"
"Magnificent conditions…unlike the players"

In common with many rural Scottish courses, *Galashiels* is not always manned. Instead players can place their green fee in an honesty box.

59

GANTON

SCARBOROUGH,
NORTH YORKSHIRE,
YO12 4PA

7TH
PAR 4 - 434 YARDS

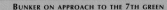

BUNKER ON APPROACH TO THE 7TH GREEN

A club's promotional literature rarely plays up the difficulty of its course deliberately. Frequently there is talk of a course being 'a fair challenge to both low and high handicappers' or some other vague claim. *Ganton* makes no apologies with its brochure positively daring you to take on the course. For instance, on arrival "there is a feeling of peace, which is broken by glimpses of the bunkers, real bunkers". In case you have not got the message: "the player who is bunkered is, rightly, punished for his error."

They have a good point. Modern bunkers are often plentiful, but they don't build them like they used to. The 7th has a nest of four bunkers on the dogleg waiting to trap short drives and the particularly vicious construction pictured overleaf to catch anything long. *Ganton's*

GANTON – BUNKER AT THE 16TH

GANTON – A GIANT BUNKER STRADDLES THE 16TH FAIRWAY

largest bunker, 75 yards wide by 50 yards long, lies 150 yards from the 16th tee and straddles the entire fairway. Golf was first played over the very rough ground at *Ganton* in 1891. In the 1930s, *Ganton's* savage yellow gorse was added and has been encouraged ever since. This provides an additional hazard to the 111 bunkers positioned aggressively around the 18 holes.

The bunkers are not the fine-sand variety found on many modern courses. Red, gritty and coarse, they are maintained so players cannot simply take a wood out and pretend they are just an extension of the fairway. The average *Ganton* bunker is 3-6ft deep with a vertical face. Many are so deep that steps are the only way in and out.

GATEHOUSE

GATEHOUSE-OF-FLEET,
DUMFRIES & GALLOWAY,
DG7 2BE

9TH
PAR 3 - 170 YARDS

9TH PLAYING DOWN A HEATHER BANK

As this hole has been the death of many rounds, it is perhaps apt that it used to be sponsored by a local undertaker. From the front tee you just about get a view of the flag, though there is no such luxury from the medal tee. Between you and the green lie 150 yards of rough and gorse (or 'whins' as they are known locally). There is no room for error to the left of the green, as anything that drifts over the dry stane dyke (stone wall) is out of bounds. The shot takes anything from an eight to a three-iron depending on the wind. Such is the height of much of the course, Hercules transport planes can sometimes be spotted in the valley below, with the Isle of Man also clearly visible across the Solway Firth.

The village of Gatehouse-of-Fleet, with its characteristic white buildings, is a haunt for fans of the cult psychological film, 'The Wicker Man', as scenes were shot there – including the exterior of the 'Green Man' Inn, in reality an estate agents. Although set in the ficticious Scottish island of Summerisle, it was actually filmed almost entirely on the mainland. It culminates in the infamous scene where Edward Woodward gets gently simmered in the locals' giant piece of basketry.

Gatehouse has a quaint wooden clubhouse, awash with colourful heather.

GATEHOUSE – LOOKING DOWN FROM 9TH TEE

GATEHOUSE'S CLUBHOUSE

5

GLEN

NORTH BERWICK,
EAST LOTHIAN,
EH39 4LE

13TH
'SEA HOLE'
PAR 3 - 135 YARDS

Though the sea provides a dramatic backdrop to a number of holes along the coast to the east of Edinburgh, rarely does it come into play in such a direct way as at *Glen*. Anything right or long from the tee ends up amongst the rocks of the Firth of Forth or, when the tide is in, a watery grave. Such is the variation in wind at the 13th's elevated tee, the hole can call for anything from a pitching wedge one day, to a three-iron the next.

The view over the green towards Bass Rock is one of the most enduring in British golf but, what players see from the tee is considerably less photogenic and more daunting, the 13th being totally blind.

BRITAIN'S MOST PICTURESQUE SEA HOLE

From the tee, the only clue is a marker post at 40 yards. Once over the brow of the hill, another 60 yards of rough must be carried before the green.

GLEN – PLAYING BLIND TO THE 13TH GREEN

GLEN – 13TH GREEN FROM THE TOP OF THE HILL

With the Bass Rock looming over the hole, the 13th is a constant favourite of TV producers and advertisers wanting to capture the ultimate Scottish coastal image, with the result that the club can expect two or three visits a year from film crews. Its frequent appearance on international TV ensure it has plenty of overseas visitors.

Aside from maintenance checks on its lighthouse, the Bass Rock has only occasional human visitors as it is far from a safe landing spot. The positioning of the 313ft high mound is an optical illusion. The shortening effect of the zoom lenses used on most published photos makes it look as though it could be reachable after a quick paddle – in fact it is a mile away from the shore. Over 100,000 sea birds are now resident. Only a few people have managed to live there, mostly by force. In darkest history, the island was a forerunner to Alcatraz. The first voluntary inhabitant was a hermit named Baldred who, in the eighth century, retreated there for some serious prayer.

THE BASS ROCK DOMINATES *GLEN*

32

GREAT YARMOUTH AND CAISTER

CAISTER-ON-SEA,
NORFOLK,
NR30 5TD

1ST

PAR 4 - 327 YARDS

The incorporation of golf courses into the centre of racetracks may seem a matter of modern commercial convenience, but *Great Yarmouth and Caister*, founded in 1882, is the second oldest club in England (after *Blackheath*) and pre-dates the racetrack. *Musselburgh Links*, East Lothian, Scotland's oldest club, contains holes both in and outside the rails of the town's racecourse but, at *Great Yarmouth and*

Caister the rails are very much in play on the first and last holes. It perhaps goes without saying that the course closes on racedays. On the 1st hole, the rails have to be crossed twice before reaching the safety of the green. The tee is situated outside the rails, requiring a drive to the inside of the course. It should then be a short-iron back over the rails as they sweep around the racetrack bend.

PLAYING OVER THE RAILS ONTO THE 1ST GREEN

Great Yarmouth and Caister is a rare example of a true English east coast links course. The club's 1982 centenary book records Thomas Browne's original proposal for a golf course on the site, in which he gives a somewhat exaggerated impression of the serene nature of the sport: "There is neither person nor circumstance in golf that can either harass, worry, excite or hurry anyone". Clearly, once the club was established he could not have landed in one of the course's gigantic sleepered bunkers – enough to give anyone a good deal of harassment and worry.

Great Yarmouth and Caister had its part in the origin of the golfing term 'bogey' to denote a score of one over par. In fact the golfing term is linked, somewhat confusingly, with two other uses of the word: the expression 'bogey man' and the character 'Colonel Bogey'. The club's founder, Thomas Browne, was dubbed 'the bogey man' by a visiting golfer (inspired by the then popular music-hall song of the same name). Browne later became a member of *Gosport*, Hampshire, where the practice was followed of addressing members by their service rank, hence, in two unlikely steps, Thomas Browne became 'Colonel Bogey'.

GREAT YARMOUTH & CAISTER – A SLEEPERED BUNKER PROTECTS THE 14TH GREEN

IT PERHAPS GOES WITHOUT SAYING THAT THE COURSE CLOSES ON RACEDAYS

GREAT YARMOUTH & CAISTER – NOT AN EASY CANTER TO MAKE THE 1ST GREEN

56

GREEN HAWORTH

ACCRINGTON,
LANCASHIRE,
BB5 3SL

4TH 'BEDLAM'
PAR 3 - 137 YARDS

PLAYING OVER THE WATER-FILLED QUARRY AT 'BEDLAM'

For sheer curiosity value alone, any hole named 'Bedlam' has to be explored. *Green Haworth* was originally a six-hole layout consisting of a rather exclusive membership confined to the family and friends of the owner. Today it is a welcoming club with nine holes playing over a series of old quarries, with ditches and a wall frequently encroaching on play.

The quarry that concentrates the mind at the 4th tee is now water-filled and, as the name suggests, can send players round the bend quite easily.

GREEN HAWORTH – 4TH TEE

GREEN HAWORTH – 2ND TEE OVER ANOTHER QUARRY

Green Haworth's charmingly named par-three 2nd, 'Jumble-holes', unnervingly plays across a rough dry quarry for most of its 118 yards. Though King of the British 'quarry courses', *Green Haworth* has some competition from *Barrow*, Cumbria, where the 8th green is situated in deep earthworks with balls liable to clatter off rocks at the back.

> A WELCOMING CLUB
> WITH NINE HOLES PLAYING
> OVER A SERIES OF
> OLD QUARRIES

HEATON PARK

PRESTWICH,
GREATER MANCHESTER,
M25 2SW

11TH
'GLEN BRACKEN'
PAR 3 - 193 YARDS

CHECK YOUR INSURANCE – VIEWERS AT
HEATON PARK'S 11TH WINTER GREEN

ACROSS THE BLOOMS AT THE 11TH

At the first sign of spring, a sizeable chunk of the population of North Manchester descends on Heaton Park, one of the area's main public attractions. At 650 acres, it is the largest municipal park in Europe. A path leads from Heaton Hall, with its mini-zoo, to the perimeter of the municipal golf course where, from a strategically placed bench, you can view players taking on one of the region's finest short holes. In fact when playing to the winter green, the public can stand within 10 yards of the flag. Though not the safest place on earth to eat an ice-cream, only the very best players trouble the pin.

HEATON PARK – TESTING TEE SHOTS OVER VALLEYS

HEATON HALL – A FAVOURITE SPOT FOR MANCUNIANS

Ex-Open champion Henry Cotton rated the 11th very highly, and it could well have the honour of Britain's best hole on a public course. From the elevated tee, there is a carry over the purple rhododendron-filled ravine with a lake below – a popular spot for apprentice fisherman. The authors have whiled away a number of hours watching players attempt the carry. About three out of four make it.

Heaton Park's par-four 12th plays back over the colourful ravine to a raised fairway. Although welcoming to players of all standards, the course is not exactly the sort of place beginners will find an easy-going introduction to the joys of the game. The course is built on a series of hills and valleys, providing some testing carries.

Nowadays, professionals can routinely carry over 300 yards from the tee. But for occasional golfers you can reduce that by about 100 yards to get into the comfort zone. We know from experience that claims of measurements on golf courses can be prone to a little exaggeration. Away from the medal tees of the Championship courses, the longest carry that has to be attempted over unplayable terrain on a British golf course is probably less than 200 yards, despite some claims to the contrary. The par-four 8th (420 yards) at *Middlesbrough*, North Yorkshire, takes some beating, where you have to clear 180 yards of shrubs and trees to reach the sanctuary of the fairway. On the 10th at *St Enodoc*, Cornwall, you can get into serious trouble if you cannot drive 200 yards over the rough.

73

HEMINGFORD ABBOTS

HUNTINGDON,
CAMBRIDGESHIRE,
PE18 9HQ

9TH

PAR 4 - 326 YARDS

THE STYLISH RAISED GREEN DESIGNED TO SEND BALLS BACK INTO THE WATER

This reasonably priced nine-hole course boasts what could easily be Britain's most 'perfect' green. The 9th at *Hemingford Abbots*, which sits within yards of the clubhouse and car park, certainly qualifies as an island green, though the depth of water in the one metre wide moat varies considerably according to the amount of rainfall. The putting area is raised like an upturned saucer with its banks sloping back into the water. After a spell of wet weather you might get lucky and have the bank hold a ball that is not quite on-target, but otherwise you can expect any errant approach to dribble agonisingly back into the drink.

> ## THE PUTTING AREA IS RAISED LIKE AN UPTURNED SAUCER WITH ITS BANKS SLOPING BACK INTO THE WATER

Being the flattest British county, Cambridgeshire is not exactly known for its hilly courses. But the intriguingly named *Gog Magog*, close to the centre of the University town, does have a touch of height, leading to the offbeat claim that if you look east from its peak, the first land that commands the same height is the Ural Mountains of Russia.

The name of *Cambridge Meridian* gives away its geographical quirk. During their round, players hop between the Eastern and Western hemispheres seven times.

Hemingford Abbots' picture-book island green is matched by an idyllic island tee for the 22nd at *Stoke Park Club*, Buckinghamshire – a hole number that might raise a few eyebrows, as the club has a choice of three layouts playing over 27 holes.

STOKE PARK CLUB'S ISLAND TEE

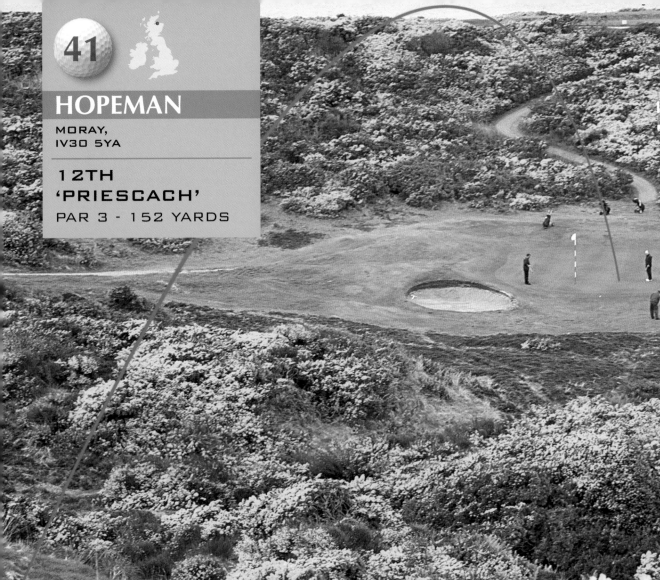

HOPEMAN

MORAY,
IV30 5YA

12TH
'PRIESCACH'

PAR 3 - 152 YARDS

THE PLUNGE FROM THE 12TH TEE

HOPEMAN – THE 12TH PLAYS BLIND FROM THE TEE

HOPEMAN – LOOKING BACK TO THE 12TH TEE

You might think that arguably the best par-three in the country comes at a price for the visiting golfer. But the green fees to play this superb drop-hole and the rest of this classic links course are amongst the lowest for a private club.

Hopeman's 'Priescach' swoops down 100ft to the green – a case of hitting and hoping for the best as, from the tee, the player gets a glimpse of the top of the specially extended flagpole but, little else that lurks below. The swirling wind coming in from the Moray Firth is of the unpredictable variety. When in the player's favour, a wedge is sufficient to find the safety of the green. When the gale is in your face, a five-wood can be a better choice.

12

ISLE OF PURBECK

SWANAGE,
DORSET,
BH19 3AB

5TH
'AGGLESTONE'

PAR 4 - 404 YARDS

5TH TEE OVERLOOKING THE HARBOUR

Many British courses attract a range of superlatives. It is safe to say that, amongst English clubs, none can boast a better aspect than the *Isle of Purbeck*. Those not familiar with the area may have difficulty getting their bearings looking at this view of the 5th from the tee.

The course occupies the Studland peninsula that juts out into the English Channel, with the holiday resort of Swanage at its head. The view over the water is actually facing north – a slight oddity for a 'south coast' hole.

The course's distinctive feature is that in mid-March it blossoms into a riot of colour. Yellow and purple gorse flowers give the 18 holes a unique feel. The view from the 5th tee was declared by King Edward VII to be amongst the finest in his kingdom. The hole plays from an elevated tee to a fairway that runs at an angle, daring you to take on as much of the rough as you think you are capable. The punishment for failure is fairly severe. Though pretty to look at, the gorse is not the sort of plant you want to be trying to get through with an eight-iron.

In 1951, Mrs Darrel-Waters was elected the club's ladies' captain. Better known under her pen name, Enid Blyton, a number of her Noddy and Big-Ears books were written in Purbeck, and she could sometimes be seen making notes outside the former clubhouse.

BOAT OF GARTEN – GULLY AT THE 15TH

The *Isle of Purbeck's* 5th is often considered to be Britian's most scenic tee and there is also an unusual consensus over the country's most scenic course. With the often snowcapped peaks of the Cairngorms dominating the area, *Boat of Garten*, Highland, comes number one on many players' lists.

But whilst admiring the scenery, players need to keep some brainpower in reserve to tackle the club's 15th. The middle of the fairway contains a deep gully from which the green is totally obscured. Rather than attempting a risky wedge out, some attempt to carry it from the tee, whilst the more cautious are content to lay

up behind it and have an uninterrupted approach shot. Former Prime Minister's husband, the late Dennis Thatcher, was a particular fan of the 15th.

The son of the first club secretary, Dan Fraser, is said to have played with only one golf ball throughout his playing days. He was aided by his small terrier, Uccu, who would sit quietly behind his master as he was playing a shot, before dashing off to lie beside the ball. Evidently his retrieving skills were a remarkable 100%. When the terrier died, Fraser never played golf again.

JEDBURGH

BORDERS,
TD8 6TA

9TH
'CHEVIOT VIEW'

PAR 4 - 309 YARDS

HIP TO BE SQUARE AT *JEDBURGH*

CONSTRUCTING AN EXTENSION TO ONE OF *JEDBURGH'S* UNUSUAL GREENS

For much of the winter season, British golfers have to make do with temporary greens; often a token effort of placing the flag at the end of the fairway in front of the normal putting area. But some courses make a special effort to construct and tend their temporary greens with as much love and care as their main surfaces. *Surbiton*, Surrey, has some particularly fine mini-winter creations, the handiwork of Tony Witt, a greenkeeper who clearly pays attention to detail.

During the 1980s' craze for artificial sporting surfaces, led by Queen's Park Rangers Football Club laying a somewhat less than natural omni-turf pitch, *Blaby*, Leicestershire, experimented with synthetic greens in an attempt to provide an all-weather putting surface. But, like the football pitches, the purists did not take to them, and *Blaby* has gone back to grass.

There are a handful of examples of courses with greens that are not the standard circular design, mostly in the wilds of the Western Isles, where it helps to cut greens into a perfect square in order that they can be fenced off from cattle and sheep.

There are no fences at *Jedburgh*, but this testing nine-hole parkland course features greens that have been shaped into perfect squares.

PERFECT WINTER GREENS AT *SURBITON*

KILLIN

**STIRLING,
FK21 8TX**

5TH 'THE DYKE'
PAR 3 - 97 YARDS

Short par-threes often present fiendish hazards to concentrate the mind but, they do not come much tougher than here at *Killin*, where the green is protected by a wall running along the length of the front edge. In keeping with the golfing tradition of rarely referring to a 'wall', the obstruction is actually called a dyke. Unhelpfully the green slopes back towards it and there is trouble on the other side with three bunkers catching anything long, left or right. A well-struck, very high lob is needed to safely clear the dyke.

5TH TEE

THE WALL PROTECTING THE GREEN

Nine-hole *Killin* has a magnificent 288-yard par-four 1st 'River', playing over an often babbling Glen Lochay as it makes its way into Loch Tay. The course is subject to invasions by deer and rabbits.

There are distinct similarities between *Killin's* 5th and the par-four 13th at *North Berwick*, where the green sits in a hollow over a stone wall.

KILLIN – 1ST OVER THE RIVER

NORTH BERWICK – 13TH PLAYING OVER A WALL TO THE GREEN

KILLIN ATTRACTS A VARIETY OF WILD ANIMALS

KIRBY MUXLOE

LEICESTERSHIRE,
LE9 2EP

5TH
PAR 4 - 297 YARDS

OUT OF BOUNDS TEE AT THE 5TH

No matter how careful your play, there is no way to avoid going out of bounds at *Kirby Muxloe*. The 5th tee is actually outside the course, one of only four British examples of the paradox of an out of bounds area being in-play. To drive back on to the course is not as easy as it might be. The tee lies in a field 80 yards from the stream that denotes the course boundary. To reach the fairway means playing through a narrow gap over a clump of trees. Having negotiated your way back, it is quite possible to go out of bounds again on your second shot as the boundary lies immediately to the left of the green.

KIRBY MUXLOE – LOOKING BACK TO THE 5TH FAIRWAY

Nearby *Whetstone*, Leicestershire, made the headlines with the convicted ball thief, Mark Collinson. It was only at the Court of Appeal that Mr Collinson's six month jail sentence for stealing balls from the lake at the course was over-turned. Although most golfers would be happy to agree that balls disappearing in to a lake can be described as abandoned, anyone tempted to don a wet suit and flippers to collect them should note, according to the judge, Mr Collinson's conditional discharge was not a 'let off' and should serve as a deterrent. We have been warned.

There is a known ball thief at *The Addington*, Surrey, who has not been reprimanded or even caught. A fox has been spotted stealing in-play balls on a number of occasions. Fortunately the ball can be replaced without penalty, as the Royal and Ancient Rule Book classes animals that steal, eat or otherwise interfere with a player's ball under the heading 'outside agency'.

34

LINDEN HALL

LONGHORSLEY,
NORTHUMBERLAND,
NE65 8XF

4TH
PAR 3 - 159 YARDS

Opened by the Duke of York in 1988, it is rumoured that the Royal visitor had a bit of a 'mare' when playing its inaugural round. The course is laid out over parkland with a variety of stunning mature trees including towering redwoods, cedars and silver birches. The casual visitor would never suspect that the course is one of the country's newest.

The 4th is a psychologically challenging par-three with four teeing areas set back from the reservoir that used to serve Linden Hall itself. The line of fire plays diagonally across the water through a narrow gap in the trees. As recompense, the green is forgivingly vast and like all at *Linden Hall* plays very true.

A TOUGH PLAY OVER WATER WITH A PERFECT GREEN WAITING

DUNHAM FOREST GOLF AND COUNTRY CLUB – PLAYING DOWN FROM RESERVOIR ON THE 16TH

One hole at *Dunham Forest Golf and County Club*, Cheshire, plays 'over' a reservoir, but there is no carry over water. The par-four 16th (400 yards) tees off from an area of land with an underground reservoir beneath it. After playing across the top of the reservoir, the fairway plunges down 25ft to a new level. Because the higher fairway section is a layer of turf on top of concrete, the drainage is not of the standard of the rest of the sweeping parkland course, so after rain it gets decidedly squishy underfoot.

Hounslow Heath, London, has a different underground feature. The only access between the two distinct areas of the course is a tunnel under a road, which at little more than 5ft high provides a slight test for claustrophobics.

A SQUEEZE TO GET TO THE NEXT HOLE AT HOUNSLOW HEATH

LLANDRINDOD WELLS

POWYS,
LD1 5NY

18TH 'DEATH OR GLORY'

PAR 4 - 297 YARDS

Difficult holes can be made even more intimidating if you have other players snapping at your heels. Thankfully, this is unlikely as you contemplate *Llandrindod Wells'* stirring finishing hole. In the heart of mid-Wales, north of the towering peaks of the Brecon Beacons, the course is rarely very busy. This is more because of its comparatively remote location than its quality, so it is very good value for your green fee.

The 18th plays across a deep valley. It is fairly risk-free to aim to pitch on to the upslope of the bank the other side, though this leaves you with a semi-blind second shot. But seeing as it is the last hole, it is a lot more satisfying to take out the timber and launch one at the road that crosses the end of the fairway, hoping to make the green for a birdie, or even better. (It has been aced). 'Death or Glory' may be the most popular hole name in Britain.

IN AND OUT OF THE VALLEY AND OVER THE ROAD

LLANDRINDOD WELLS – 18TH TEE

The 'death' on this hole is not as messy as in many 'Death or Glory' holes. The biggest headache is pitching directly onto the road. Such a hard landing tends to shoot the ball straight off the back of the green and into the trees.

Painswick, Gloucestershire, features a delightful road hole, the 17th, where players can actually find themselves playing over a junction. To check the road is clear, there is a lookout tower at the tee.

PAINSWICK – 17TH OVER MINOR ROADS

Llanymynech, Shropshire, is another special course in Wales...or is it? It is laid out with 15 of its 18 holes in Wales and the remainder in England. There is even one hole, the 4th, where the golfer tees off in Wales to a green in England.

71

LOCH NESS

INVERNESS,
HIGHLAND,
IV2 3XQ

14TH 'CHANCE'
PAR 3 - 76 YARDS

At 6772 yards, *Loch Ness* is one of the lengthier Scottish layouts, which makes it all the more surprising that its signature hole weighs in at a tiny 76 yards. A stream runs through the middle of the course and is played over twice, at the 2nd and on this one-shotter, the 14th. From the tee, the ground drops away into a 30ft gully with trees and foliage. The slope is just as steep up the other side to the green. The leafy nature of the hole is characteristic of *Loch Ness*, well-known for its lush, green feel.

PLAYING OVER THE GULLY AT THE SHORT **14TH**

LOCH NESS – 14TH GREEN

LOCH NESS – FROM 14TH TEE

There is plenty of room for large creepy-crawlies in Loch Ness itself. To give some golfing scale of its depth you would have to play the 14th at *Loch Ness* golf course more than four times vertically downwards until you would hit the bottom.

LOCH NESS

Computer technology has largely made the chilly business of hanging around the loch waiting for Nessie's rare appearances unnecessary. Click onto *www.lochness.co.uk/livecam* and it is possible to keep up a vigil without leaving your laptop. The best, though not perhaps the most exciting of explanations, is that the visual 'disturbances' on the loch are caused by dead trees that having rested on the bottom for years become engorged with gas. This causes them to rise dramatically to the top vaguely resembling a prehistoric creature surfacing.

82

LOCHCARRON

**HIGHLAND,
IV54 8YU**

**1ST
'JOHNNY'S SEAT'
PAR 3 – 210 YARDS**

Perhaps the most variable British water hazard, the 1st not only allows scenic views across the expanse of Loch Carron but, depending on the tide, the loch frequently encroaches on play. Even at low water, the burn that winds across the hole at 150-200 yards tends to gobble up tee shots for which there is a long-handled ball-scoop attached to the bridge.

Things start to get really interesting on the nine-hole course when the tide comes in. Although the green itself generally escapes the flood, just about everything else between tee and green disappears under water. To improve the footing on the bridge, the club had the idea of laying down old tee mats. But this had to be abandoned as the greenkeeper grew tired of taking his tractor up and down the shore in search of mats that had been washed away.

1ST AT HIGH TIDE

**DEPENDING ON THE TIDE, THE LOCH FREQUENTLY
ENCROACHES ON PLAY**

The area is a mecca for 'Munro baggers' (climbers who set out to scale Britain's highest mountains), with 12 peaks of at least 3000ft within easy reach of the small village of Lochcarron. To drive to the nearest town, Inverness, takes as long as from London to Birmingham (depending on the traffic).

The picture postcard course of similarly named *Lochranza*, to the south on the Isle of Arran, is also well-known for its tendency to succumb to tidal forces. In spring, huge rainstorms can swell the incoming tide engulfing the whole course though, within two hours, the waters can subside and play recommence as though nothing has happened.

LOCHCARRON – 1ST AT LOW TIDE

LOCHCARRON – TO COMPLETE THE SET...NEITHER HIGH NOR LOW TIDE

The media descended en masse on the Highlands for the wedding of Madonna and Guy Ritchie at Dornoch Church, running up a bill of £250,000 for accommodation alone. Photographers scoured every ironmonger in the area for stepladders, used to get a vantage point to snap the happy couple. After the event, dozens were left abandoned on the roadside – now stored by locals in their garden sheds and ready to be put to a more worthwhile use.

35

LONG ASHTON

CLARKEN COOMBE,
SOMERSET,
BS41 9DW

2ND
PAR 3 - 126 YARDS

If you could take every interesting par-three feature you could possibly think of and throw them together in a single hole, you would end up with something similar to this glorious one-shotter. The 2nd at *Long Ashton* has nearly everything. From a high tee, the ground immediately falls away sharply to a minor road complete with a set of overhead cables to contend with. The small green sits at the base of a quarry, with a vertical rock face shrouding the left-hand side. Inevitably, many clatter straight into the limestone with unpredictable consequences.

THE FEATURE PACKED 2ND FROM THE TEE

LOOKING BACK TO THE 2ND TEE

Long Ashton's tree-lined parkland course is known for the luxurious carpet-like feel of its fairways, aided by excellent drainage that makes it playable even in the toughest of winter conditions. Since its formation in 1893, the layout has been subject to a series of adjustments. Negotiations over the purchase of the 14 acre plot between the current 7th and 8th holes progressed in a stately fashion. Discussions started between the club and local farmer, Mr Withers, in 1962.

They finally shook hands on the deal thirty years later.

LONG ASHTON – 'BENNETT'S GAP' IN THE 18TH FAIRWAY

The obstacles in the middle of the 2nd fairway at *Lundin Ladies*, Fife, are less movable. Believed to be the oldest club that allows only ladies as members, the course is renowned for its three stalks of rock, 'The Standing Stones', that date back around 4000 years. For most of the 20th century, they were shrouded in a fence and were consequently regarded as immovable obstructions from which players could obtain relief. However after a ruling by the Ancient Monuments Board for Scotland the fence was taken down, making the stones an integral part of the course. Whilst dignifying them, this means that anyone finding that the rocks impede their shot must cope the best they can.

If you find a particular feature of a course a little too challenging, there is the remote option of trying to get the club to remove it. This happened at *Long Ashton* in 1957 when club President, Joe Bennett, became frustrated at the number of times he got stuck behind a bank in the 18th fairway. The offending obstacle was built by soldiers during the First World War. In exchange for a new carpet for the clubhouse, the Green Committee agreed to make a hole in the bank. 'Bennett's Gap' remains to this day to aid progress up the 18th fairway.

LUNDIN LADIES – 'THE STANDING STONES' ON THE 2ND FAIRWAY

Occasionally, obstacles are mysteriously removed without a club's knowledge. Nobody knows who took a pickaxe to conifers on the 9th at *Tillicoultry Golf Club*, near Stirling, in 2002. Suspicions remain that it may have been a rogue member taking drastic action to make the hole easier.

67

THE MACHRIE

ISLE OF ISLAY,
NORTH AYRSHIRE,
PA42 7AN

17TH
IFRINN

PAR 4 - 352 YARDS

NOT EXACTLY STRAIGHTFORWARD TO READ A PUTT ON THE 17TH

The Machrie may be the most difficult British course for the first-time player but, once navigated, it becomes a favourite of all who play there. The initial difficulty is that the course is laid out amongst vast sand dunes, meaning an unusually large number of blind shots. In fact, playing to its par of 71, 12 of a player's 35 full shots are liable to be completely blind.

Barring some minor changes in the 1970s, the course is set out in the same way as when the British Open was held there in 1901 – the first Championship where the prize money reached a princely three figures.

The 17th's name, 'Ifrinn', is Gaelic for 'hell', appropriate as the par-four plays onto a ridge from the tee followed by a mid-iron over another of the course's characteristic hills. As is often the case with diabolically difficult approach shots, there is little respite when the green is finally reached. The 17th is possibly the most topsy-turvy undulating green in the country.

You can take your pick from any number of feature holes at *The Machrie*. The approach to the 7th green, however, must rank as one of the most unnerving blind shots anywhere. Aiming for a solitary marker post, a 30ft hillock has to be cleared, to avoid dense rough on landing.

THE MACHRIE – THE 7TH THE KING OF BLIND HOLES

The Isle of Islay (pronounced Eye-la) is not always the wild, windswept place that mainlanders might believe. However on the occasions when conditions get testing, the course has a reputation for bordering on the unplayable. But generally the climate is actually quite mild, contributing to the fact that the turf at *The Machrie* is amongst the most lush and springy of any British golf course, provided you can actually manage to keep the ball on any of the fairways.

AN UNUSUALLY LARGE NUMBER OF BLIND SHOTS

33

MACHRIHANISH

ARGYLL & BUTE,
PA28 6PT

1ST 'BATTERY'

PAR 4 - 428 YARDS

THE MOST BRACING OPENING HOLE IN THE COUNTRY

MACHRIHANISH – 1ST LOOKING BACK TOWARDS THE TEE

MACHRIHANISH – 1ST GREEN

Definitely not the course to jump onto the 1st tee without a few limbering-up exercises. The sensible option here is to try to carry about 150 yards across the bay to reach the 1st fairway, though the bullish attempt to take on considerably more. The 1st doglegs slightly left with the fairway tight against the beach along its length.

Britain's coastal scenes are constantly evolving. Whilst eastern England's coastlines are threatening to fall into the sea, on the west coast of Kintyre things are moving the other way. Around 50 years ago there was far more sand around the coast of the bay. Now the grass is gradually encroaching on the beach. *Machrihanish's* 16th 'Rorke's Drift' was, in times past, played almost entirely over sand with wooden planks for golfers to walk on. Today the links are of Championship standard, with the dunes providing many blind shots.

There is plenty of agreement that *Machrihanish* has Britain's most formidable (and brazen) opening hole. But for a gentler warm-up to your round, try the slightly more forgiving 1st at *Cleeve Hill*, Gloucestershire. The course, playing across the beacon overlooking Cheltenham racecourse, features an opener with a gigantic fairway so wide that a short par-four could probably play over its width.

MAGDALENE FIELDS

BERWICK-UPON-TWEED,
NORTHUMBERLAND,
TD15 1NE

8TH
'GOOD LUCK'
PAR 3 - 160 YARDS

OVER THE DOOMY 120FT DEEP INLET

MAGDALENE FIELDS – 8TH TEE ACROSS THE INLET

Magdalene Fields (pronounced like it is spelt, unlike the eccentric 'Maud-lin' Oxford College version) is a public course – so for less than £20, visitors are welcome at any time to take on the challenge of one of the country's most incredible sea holes.

LINING UP TO TAKE ON *MAGDALENE FIELDS* ' 8TH

Possibly the most subdued description of any hole in Britain appears on the website for *Magdalene Fields*: 'the 8th requires an accurate tee-shot over the cove'. Although not the longest carry over the sea in the country, *Magdalene Fields*' inlet must be the deepest, most forbidding golf hazard in the Britain. The 8th ranks as one of the great 'lost' golfing experiences. Neither the hole nor the club has made many appearances in the golfing 'Top 100' lists that do the rounds but instead have remained remarkably anonymous.

Making the carry over the 120ft deep cove is no guarantee of success. The rough from the green leading down over the cliff is extremely steep. Such is the danger to golfers that the whole area is out of bounds meaning, that even if you do clear the gap, you still risk picking up a penalty. The flag – just visible as a yellow dot in our picture – is positioned on a heavily bunker-protected green (just in case you felt that the drive across the ocean was a bit routine).

MAGDALENE FIELDS' INLET MUST BE THE DEEPEST, MOST FORBIDDING GOLF HAZARD IN BRITAIN

63

MANNINGS HEATH

WEST SUSSEX,
RH13 6PG

10TH
PAR 3 - 169 YARDS

PAR-THREE OVER THE WATERFALL

It comes as something of a relief to report a British course that is not constantly buffeted by high winds. *Mannings Heath's* two courses are comparatively sheltered from the elements by the mature trees lining the fairways. The gently sloping Waterfall Course plays through a variety of parkland, heath and wooded areas, with an 'English country garden' short 10th. Playing over a stream with the waterfall gurgling to your right, there is an 80ft drop down to the two-tiered green. The cottage is, of course, out of bounds so there is not a lot of room for error long.

MANNINGS HEATH – AVOIDING THE STREAMS FROM THE TEE ON THE 11TH

MANNINGS HEATH – 11TH GREEN THROUGH THE BLUEBELL WOOD

The 368-yard par-four 11th, included in Gary Player's list of the best 18 holes, meanders its way through a wooded valley with a stream ready to swallow anything to the left. During the Second World War, a bomber crashed on the par-three 14th. Since then poppies have flowered on the site.

The course is subject to one of the country's odd postcode anomalies. Instead of referring to a large regional population centre, much of rural Sussex is lumbered with the RH prefix of Redhill, a small commuter town in Surrey.

MANOR HOUSE

CASTLE COMBE,
WILTSHIRE,
SN14 7JW

17TH
'BURTON BROOK'
PAR 3 - 151 YARDS

LOOKING DOWN FROM TEE TO DOUBLE-GREEN OF THE 17TH

MANOR HOUSE – MULTIPLE HAZARDS AT THE **18TH**

where you put your drive on this par-four, the approach shot is still going to be tough. Five bunkers surround the green, trees are too close for comfort on the left and three interconnecting lakes (with waterfalls) guard the right.

The Manor House Hotel, now a luxury leisure complex, takes some beating as the spookiest looking building in Britain. One particular room is known for a ghost that appears only to mothers. The current housekeeper reported having her hair pulled by the phantom. There are plenty of strange goings-on in Castle Combe village as well. The Castle Inn is said to have had a curse put on it, causing the odd side-effect of making CD players jump. It probably makes Chris de Burgh albums sound a lot better.

Whilst scouring the country for extraordinary golf holes, we were often asked 'have you got *Manor House?*' making it the most recommended course in our collection. The course winds its way through an ancient wooded valley close to the outskirts of the 14th century village of Castle Combe, a contender for Britain's prettiest village.

There are plenty of amazing holes to choose from but the vertigo-inducing 17th is a particularly breathtaking drop-hole and, at 130ft, is one of the country's biggest height differences between tee and green. Unusually, the 17th has two greens, used alternately. Both have their downsides. The left-hand green is larger but more undulating and is protected by three bunkers, with a brook behind. There are no bunkers on the right green but the brook catches anything short.

The 18th at *Manor House* has a deserved reputation for being Britain's most picturesque closing hole. It doesn't really matter

THE MANOR HOUSE HOTEL

MATFEN HALL

MATFEN,
NORTHUMBERLAND,
NE20 0RH

2ND
PAR 4 - 292 YARDS

Ramparts and various types of fortification play a part in many of the more interesting layouts but a defensive feature of a quite different nature comes into play at *Matfen Hall*.

The course, constructed in 1995, occupies the parkland grounds of the magnificent country house, dating from 1830. Running through the estate is a 5ft high 'ha-ha' to prevent livestock from roaming too near the house. Rather than constructing a simple wall, the landscapers cut into the ground in order to provide a change in elevation of the land. Stones were built up on the side of the bank that faces away from the house. The jump up to the higher level was beyond the abilities of cattle and sheep and the views of the Hall's 19th century inhabitants were not spoilt by an unsightly wall.

OVER THE 'HA-HA' TO THE 2ND GREEN

The 'ha-ha' comes into play on the 11th and short par-five 13th, where it crosses the fairway 20 yards before the green. But on the par-four 2nd, the small green has been built up immediately behind it on a bank providing a significant elevation change to the approach shot. If you land just in front of the 'ha-ha', don't get fantasies of being allowed a free drop: it is a permanent feature from which there is no relief.

MATFEN HALL – THE 'HA-HA' AT CLOSE QUARTERS

CHARNWOOD FOREST – CLEAR THE BROOK THEN AVOID THE WALL ON THE 4TH

Matfen Hall certainly warrants an entry for the most obscure feature of any British golf course. Despite attempts to find out its origin, nobody really knows why the 18th fairway is adorned with a mysterious stone pyramid. The best guess is that it functioned as a store in the 19th century.

MATFEN HALL'S MYSTERIOUS PYRAMID

CHARNWOOD FOREST – LOOKING BACK TO FAIRWAY WALL ON THE 4TH

Also bisected with walls is the nine-hole *Charnwood Forest*, Leicestershire. The course plays round outcrops of 800 million year old granite 'Hanginstone' rocks, with the additional hazard of a 5ft high stone wall coming into play at two holes. On the 285-yard par-four 4th you play over a brook onto a rising fairway that, 50 yards before the green, has a wall running straight across it.

72

MOFFAT

DUMFRIES & GALLOWAY,
DG10 9SB

9TH
'PORT ARTHUR'
PAR 3 - 134 YARDS

CLEARING THE CLIFF OF 'PORT ARTHUR'

BEST NOT TO GET STUCK HALFWAY UP *MOFFAT'S* 9TH

At *Moffat*, golfers on the 7th tee know that it is worth making a mental note of the position of the flag at the 9th otherwise, within a few minutes, they will have very little idea where they are supposed to be hitting.

The word 'intimidating' features heavily in the golfers' lexicon but this par-three needs no overstatement. From the tee, the ground rises – gently at first – before developing into a towering rock face. A lonely marker post at the top is the solitary indication of where to aim. Fluff it from the tee and things rapidly get worse as, the nearer the face you get, the steeper and more blind the recovery shot becomes.

The origin of the hole's name, 'Port Arthur', is delightfully obscure. It may derive from the principal base of the Russian Eastern Fleet during the Russo-Japanese War of 1904 (the course opened in the same year), whose main defence was the amphitheatre of hills surrounding the port.

66

MONMOUTH

MONMOUTHSHIRE,
NP25 3SN

8TH
'CRESTA RUN'
PAR 4 - 450 YARDS

THE S-SHAPED FAIRWAY FROM THE 8TH TEE

LOOKING BACK UP THE 8TH FAIRWAY

For its affordable visitors' green fees, *Monmouth* wins our prize for the best value club in the country. For less than half that charged by most private courses, you can enjoy this scenic South Wales course and take the challenge of an unusual, long par-four: one with a double dogleg.

At 450 yards, the 'Cresta Run' is bordering par-five status but is made even more difficult by a fairway that takes one turn, and then promptly heads back the other way. From the tee, the fairway sweeps away down into the valley. But a well-placed drive comes up against a huge clump of evergreens at one edge of a farm that occupies the centre of the course. If you unleash a belting drive, it is possible to cut the corner and make it to the green in two. But mortals tend to aim their second shot to the right of the trees, leaving a chip onto the green so settling for a five.

Monmouth also plays host to a particularly satisfying drop-hole. The par-three 2nd 'Cannes Folly' (180 yards) plays over the road to the farm in the valley. Anything hooked ends up in the donkey paddock but there is little trouble at the back of the green so there is no reason to hold back. Although the actual gradient is not the steepest we came across, the difference in height from tee to green is an immense 150ft.

MONMOUTH – LOOKING BACK UP TO THE 2ND TEE

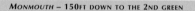
MONMOUTH – 150FT DOWN TO THE 2ND GREEN

In 1996, *Monmouth Golf Club* celebrated its centenary. Amongst the reminiscences of its members is Mr D M R Jenkins' admission that, when trying to escape from the bunker on the 4th, he managed to play the shot into the back of his own neck; a feat achieved because he diligently kept his head down – as all the instruction manuals recommend – unaware that the ball had hit the lip of the bunker and flipped backwards, before coming down vertically.

Monmouth is easily confused with nearby *Rolls of Monmouth* and *Monmouthshire* in Abergavenny. There is also *West Monmouthshire*, home of Britain's highest tee, where the 14th sits 1513ft above sea level.

49

MORAY

LOSSIEMOUTH,
MORAY,
IV31 6QS

18TH
PAR 4 - 406 YARDS

The Scottish links courses are famed for their humps and undulations, the ultimate example being this finishing hole on the Old Course at *Moray*. Teeing off close to a row of houses as the course makes its way back into the centre of Lossiemouth, the fairway weaves its way through a series of grassy mounds. One of the dunes that runs through the spine of the playing area is 20 yards long. The green is placed in a natural amphitheatre, protected by an infamous 'hell's bunker'.

Inevitably, for a hole that skirts to the side of peoples' gardens, many players stray out of bounds on the right. One particularly vulnerable house is owned by a builder who enjoys a round or two of golf himself. According to local folklore, he has not had to buy a golf ball since 1946.

THE UNDULATIONS ON THE APPROACH TO THE 18TH GREEN

THE SCOTTISH LINKS COURSES ARE FAMED FOR THEIR HUMPS AND UNDULATIONS

MORAY – ONE OF THE MANY MOUNDS ON THE **18**TH

MORAY – AMPHITHEATRE GREEN ON THE **18**TH

Shortly after the club's formation, Ramsay MacDonald became a member of *Moray* but was expelled for holding pacifist views, causing heated debate amongst members of the time. On becoming the first Labour Prime Minister, he was invited to rejoin though, not surprisingly, he declined the offer.

Littlestone, Kent, was, around the same time, the scene of an unusually cosy political alliance. In 1908, its captain was the then Prime Minister Herbert Asquith who, no doubt never had a cross word with the club's President – Arthur Balfour, the leader of the opposition.

In the present day, there are surprisingly few senior British politicians bitten with the golf bug. Tony Blair did complete four holes with Bill Clinton but more as a photo-call than a serious sporting endeavour. He is said to have three-putted on all four of them.

MUTHILL

**PERTH AND KINROSS,
PH5 2DA**

13TH
'LAVEROCK LEA'
PAR 4 - 291 YARDS

The most imposing tee in the country is generally acknowledged to be the 9th at the Ailsa Course at *Turnberrry*, balanced on a rocky outcrop with Atlantic waves crashing below. The only crashing you are likely to hear at the 13th tee at *Muthill* is the greenkeeper falling over his pitchfork. However, it certainly warrants an entry as the most unusual tee position in Britain. Following the development of the tee area for the 13th all of the club's nine holes now play from two different teeing positions. To complete the job of providing a new challenge on each of its nine holes, the club made a tee for the 13th – playing straight over a tractor shed! Because of its slightly raised position, it allows for a satisfying open-shouldered drive. But you have to take pity on any employee working inside when a

13TH OVER THE TRACTOR SHED

player does not quite manage the necessary loft. The green in the foreground belongs to the 3rd/12th. The 13th hole plays to the left of our picture, before doglegging right to a flag that appears almost to be back on the 3rd/12th fairway.

MUTHILL – THE TINY GREEN AT THE 18TH

There is compensation for *Muthill's* tight fairways. The turf is amongst the best for an inland course, being of the golfer-friendly super-springy variety and the rough is not excessive. But the greens are very small with the 9th/18th (202 yards, par-three) challenging to be the tiniest (non-winter) green on a senior British course.

A former club captain, Joe Connaghan, submitted a claim to be included in the Guinness Book of Records for a freaky run of scores at the beginning of a round. He started with a hole-in-one, a decent feat in itself, and then followed with a two at the second, a three at the third....all the way to a double bogey-six at the sixth. With his score card reading 1,2,3,4,5,6 for the first six holes, it set some sort of precedent for declaring the same score as the hole number. The people from Guinness were not utterly convinced that he was really trying as hard as he could when getting his six, and turned it down.

MUTHILL – NOT MUCH TO AIM FOR ON THE 18TH

NEFYN AND DISTRICT

MORFA NEFYN,
GWYNEDD,
LL53 6DA

13TH
PAR 4 - 415 YARDS

The green at the end of the world is an apt description of the 13th on the Old Course at *Nefyn and District*. Holes 12 to 17 play up a narrow peninsula where, close to the 13th tee, the land is just 30 yards across. The tee is offset to the left of the strip of land, meaning a first shot across the cliff in line with a marker post; though there is the safe option of aiming well to the right and trying to make up the ground later.

The green is at the furthest point of the peninsula, with a very narrow entrance protected by rocks and, of course, the Atlantic for those who stray wildly left, right or long.

TAKE ON SOME OF THE PENINSULA FROM THE 13TH TEE

NEFYN AND DISTRICT – 13TH GREEN AT THE END OF THE PENINSULA

The sea can be seen from every single hole at *Nefyn and District*, and there are plenty of them. The course had 18 holes in 1912 before a further nine were added in 1933. There are currently 26 – a front 10 and two completely different back eights.

Nefyn and District boasts its very own 'Old Faithful' on the par-five 12th (478 yards). Before you reach the green there is a blow-hole with a 100ft drop down to the sea, which occasionally showers the course with water to the alarm of unsuspecting players.

NEFYN AND DISTRICT – BLOW-HOLE GUARDING THE APPROACH TO THE 12TH

55

NEWBURGH-ON-YTHAN

NEWBURGH,
ABERDEENSHIRE,
AB41 6BE

4TH 'DROVERS'
PAR 4 - 285 YARDS

BEST TO PLAY UP OR TO THE RIGHT OF THE RUIN

Newburgh-on-Ythan is another club that purchased nearby land to extend from nine to eighteen holes which, in the case of this coastal course, was as recently as 1996. You might imagine that a hole featuring the ruins of an old house must surely have been part of the original layout. In fact, despite its feel of antiquity, the 4th was part of the outward nine that was added only a few years ago.

NEWBURGH-ON-YTHAN – 4TH GREEN LOOKING BACK TO THE RUIN

courses and, if avoiding the peak of high season, you are not exactly going to be fighting to get on the first tee. When visiting clubs in the area in May, we were astonished how deserted many were, compared to the throngs further south.

———————

But for those in the south-east who cannot make the trip, there are a number of English courses that have a strangely Scottish feel. *Piltdown*, with its purplish heather and bracken gives the illusion that you are 400 miles north, though it is actually only eight miles from the south coast in East Sussex.

In theory, the hole should present a great birdie opportunity. Playing from a raised tee, it is a reasonably short par-four. But whilst it might look possible to skirt the ruin altogether to the left, the area is the out of bounds of the 3rd fairway.

Newburgh-on-Ythan's ruins are the remains of an old house that was an overnight stop for drovers transferring their herds. Today there are just three walls left that, at 3-4ft high, sit in the middle of the fairway 200 yards from the tee. The gap where the door was is still evident. The best line to the green is somewhere behind or to the right of the walls. They are classed as immovable obstructions, so there is no relief if you start sending balls pinging around the drovers' front room.

Despite the Welsh ring to *Newburgh-on-Ythan's* name, it is in the heart of Scottish golfing country, 10 miles south of Cruden Bay. This region around Aberdeenshire and Moray is particularly well represented in our collection. Base yourself anywhere in this area and you can get to choose between a host of great value

> **THE RUINS ARE THE REMAINS OF AN OLD HOUSE THAT WAS AN OVERNIGHT STOP FOR DROVERS**

PILTDOWN – A TASTE OF SCOTLAND IN THE SOUTH OF ENGLAND

5TH
PAR 4 - 369 YARDS

THE 5TH FAIRWAY IS DIVIDED BY A STREAM

CHOOSE WHICH SIDE TO GO ON THE 5TH

Such was the care lavished on the construction of this course in 1993 that it was left to mature a full two years before anyone was permitted to play a round. The 5th is bordered on its right by a stream along virtually its complete length. There is another stream down the left-hand side and, just for good measure, one that runs straight down the middle of the fairway effectively cutting it in half. The middle stream is not exactly a tiny trickle either. At 12ft wide, it is best to make a clear decision from the tee which side you intend to go. Three bridges positioned at strategic points along the double-fairway help players taking a zig-zag line to the green.

Norfolk's greens are maintained to USGA specification and in the case of the 9th, there is an awful lot of

NORFOLK – 1000 SQUARE YARD GREEN ON THE 9TH

green to maintain. The putting surface of the 184-yard par-three hole measures 53 yards from tip to tip, giving it an area of over 1000 square yards, though they do not make it too easy, as two of the largest bunkers on the course loom at its front. The 'average' sized British green, if there is such a thing, probably measures about half the size. The club is prepared to make the claim that it is the largest in the county and it must be in running for the

biggest green for a single hole in the country. (The Old Course at St Andrews features a number of enormous double-greens).

We have not had our tape measures out but challengers include Kingsbarns, Fife, where the 15th has a gigantic pear-shaped green balanced on the shoreline and the huge 18th at Keith, North Ayrshire.

52

NORTH BERWICK

EAST LOTHIAN,
EH39 4BB

16TH 'GATE'
PAR 4 - 381 YARDS

THE GULLY IN THE 16TH GREEN

Only *St Andrews* has continuously staged golf longer than *North Berwick*. A true links course, its curves and undulations are the work of the North Sea over many centuries. Incorporating features that modern designers probably would not dare to propose, the course throws up every conceivable hazard: walls in play, the Firth of Forth and bunkers the size of small quarries.

North Berwick could occupy a volume of 'Extra-ordinary Golf Holes' on its own but, undoubtedly, the 16th possesses the most amazing green in the country. The flag can be positioned either side of a 6ft deep gully – allowing the rare golfing horror of a 'blind' putt should your ball roll into it.

NORTH BERWICK'S MUCH COPIED 15TH

Standing on the 15th tee gives a fair impression of why 'Redan' has so many admirers. Over-clubbing is dangerous as a stone wall sits a mere 10 yards behind the green. But it is the challenge nearest to you that is liable to concentrate the mind. Two formidable bunkers protecting the front of the green appear to stand almost vertically. But even finding the right distance from the tee is no guarantee of par, as the green is full of slopes and borrows that make three-putting a risk even from near the pin. *North Berwick's* car park is particularly vulnerable to stray drives from the 18th. Such is the number of windscreens that get assaulted the club sells daily car damage insurance for 50p.

North Berwick's golfing geography is not so easy to navigate. Not to be confused with Berwick-upon-Tweed, 25 miles down the coast, North Berwick lies to the east of Edinburgh, and plays host to two courses, *North Berwick* and *Glen* (the latter is sometimes referred to as the East Links at North Berwick). You might imagine that it was North Berwick Golf Club who played at *North Berwick* golf course … but no such luck. It is shared by the Tantallon and Bass Rock Golf Clubs.

North Berwick's signature hole 'Redan' has claims to be the most copied on earth – the design of the short 15th (192 yards) is said to be the inspiration for 16 other courses, many in the USA. Three of them manage to recreate the exact yardage: the 3rd at *Ocean Links*, Rhode Island, the 6th at *Fox Chapel Golf Club*, Philadelphia and the 15th at the Jack Nicklaus-designed *Prospector Course*, Arizona.

NORTH BERWICK – CAVERNOUS BUNKER AT THE 15TH

INTO THE DUNES AT 'O.L.'

NORTH WALES – BLIND FROM THE 16TH TEE

North Wales features a mix of holes. The first seven have a traditional parkland feel; whereas the remaining 11, playing through the rolling dunes, are classic links material. South of the border, many links courses are not easily accessible to visiting golfers. Although it is best to let them know in advance, *North Wales* is welcoming to holidaymakers and is a good bet to get a taste of genuine links action.

> ## THE GREEN IS HIDDEN WITHIN A LARGE BOWL OF DUNES

N orth Wales, which caters for holiday golfers visiting Llandudno, is built on church land. This caused slight friction when the club named their 16th 'Oh Hell'. In an attempt to appease the landlords, the 18th was given a rather more tranquil biblical title, 'Paradise'. To tone it down further, 'Oh Hell', became 'O.L.'

In fact the view from the tee of this blind par-three is liable to make you utter a considerably stronger expletive. The front of the green is protected by two huge humps that prevent any real sight of the target area from the tee. When the wind howls it is not unknown for the hole to need a driver. The green is hidden within a large bowl of dunes, the banks of which are not the sort that let the ball roll sedately to the green, being covered with spindly gorse.

Steps lead up the largest dune to the 17th tee, another short, testing par-three, this time called 'L.O.' Playing over the 17th's line of fire, there is another semi-hidden green to go for.

NORTH WALES – 17TH TEE

40

NORTHCLIFFE

SHIPLEY,
WEST YORKSHIRE,
BD18 4LJ

1ST
PAR 4 - 250 YARDS

THE PARKLAND CHASM OF THE 1ST

NORTHCLIFFE'S 18TH WITH ITS GREEN 'UNDER' THE 1ST

Often the entrance to a golf course gives a good indication as to what lies within. The gates to *Northcliffe* perch on a one-in-four gradient on the road leading from Shipley, following a near-hairpin bend. The drop the other side of the clubhouse is just as sharp, producing one of the most dramatic opening holes in the north of England.

The teeing areas for the 1st hug the clubhouse closely, possibly a little too closely for those visitors nervous of playing their opening shot in public, as the scene that greets you from the 1st tee is an uneasy mix of the idyllic and the horrific. The green in the chasm is the 18th. The 1st plays over the top of it and, all being well, onto the ridge the other side. Thankfully, you are not expected to clamber down and back up again – an impressive iron bridge takes you across the gap. When we visited, most seemed content to play an iron from the tee but the bold can take out a wood and opt to go for the 200-yard carry over the gap and a clump of trees to the left of the dogleg fairway.

Northcliffe's signature hole is the 177-yard par-three 18th. A stream runs down its entire length with trees left and right. At the green you can glance up and see players at the opener attempting to clear the ravine, hitting over your head ... if you're lucky.

THE SCENE THAT GREETS YOU FROM THE 1ST TEE IS AN UNEASY MIX OF THE IDYLLIC AND THE HORRIFIC

OKEHAMPTON

DEVON,
EX20 1EF

12TH
PAR 3 - 90 YARDS

Many of the country's most intriguing lay-outs spring from the fact that an original nine-hole course has later been extended to eighteen. *Okehampton*, clinging to a hillside on the north-western boundary of Dartmoor National Park, opened in 1913. Just seven years later it was lengthened to its present format. In places, the added holes weave ingeniously through the original layout, with the 10th and 15th playing from different directions to a double-green.

Tucked away in the furthest corner of the course, the 12th is amongst the country's steepest and most forbidding drop-holes. The wooden teeing area nestles within a thick bank of trees, with the flag only partly visible. The back of the green is guarded by the River Okement but a par here is doubly tricky as *Okehampton's* greens are perilously fast with plenty of dips and borrows to overcome.

THE 12TH'S 'PARALLEL BARS' TEEING AREA

Okehampton's extended layout does not make it especially tight, whereas some clubs glory in their ability to fit a senior course into a small area. *Kingsthorpe*, Northampton, claims the prize for compactness with its 5918-yard eighteen-hole parkland course occupying just 73 acres.

> THE 12TH IS AMONGST THE COUNTRY'S STEEPEST AND MOST FORBIDDING DROP-HOLES

THE DROP TO THE 12TH GREEN

THE TIGHT SIX-HOLE LAYOUT AT *CASTLEFIELDS*, WEST YORKSHIRE

But for the sheer 'ahhh' factor, you need to visit *Castlefields*, West Yorkshire. Celebrating its centenary in 2003, the club squeezes in six par-three holes that are played three times to make a round of 18 – the longest being 171 yards. Between the two furthest points the boundaries of the course are little more than 200 yards apart, meaning that all the holes play over each other. The fact that the 1st plays over the line of four other holes is surely a claim for uniqueness.

Castlefields' minutes contain the traditional pearls of golfing history. At the 1969 Annual General Meeting, the captain finished his report by stating that "a large supply of Bramshaw Pork Pies were available". The following year it was noted that "Mr Sands said he enjoyed the pies provided" and, if this continued for future committee meetings, "he would make a point of being there".

50

ORSETT

ESSEX,
RM16 3DS

14TH 'COTTAGE'
PAR 4 - 358 YARDS

PROTECTIVE MEASURES AT THE COTTAGE HOLE

ORSETT – 14TH WITH A HOUSE IN PLAY

At least for one feature *Orsett* has a distinct similarity to the Old Course at *St Andrews*, as both have an inhabited building coming into play. *Orsett's* cottage has a lot more aesthetic appeal than the modern wing of the hotel that impinges onto *St Andrews'* 17th fairway.

Britain's most vulnerable golfing house lies to one side of the fairway on *Orsett's* 14th, protected by a six metre wire mesh. The house became stranded in the middle of the course when the layout was increased from 9 to 18 holes. Anything from the tee with a touch of draw brings the house very much into play, with the occupants enduring endless approach shots straight over their roof. The course pays for any damage to roof tiles or windows. The same family have lived there for 25 years, so presumably enjoy their unique location.

Wellingborough, Northamptonshire, has a magnificent stately home as a clubhouse and one of the outbuildings, a gazebo, manages to come into play. *Moatlands*, Kent, has a Victorian bath house that needs to be avoided on its 10th. Many British tee areas have had to be enclosed within netting to prevent stray drives from finding their way into houses that border the golf course. The most dramatic piece of defensive civil engineering is probably at *Airlinks*, London, where the 12th and 13th tees are virtually surrounded by netting to stop drives flying into the road.

Close to *Orsett*, at *Royal Epping Forest*, Essex, there is a bye-law guaranteed to catch out casual visitors. All players must wear red garments.

AVOIDING *WELLINGBOROUGH'S* GAZEBO FROM THE TEE

54

THE OXFORDSHIRE

MILTON COMMON,
OXFORDSHIRE,
OX9 2PU

17TH
'TREBLE CHANCE'
PAR 5 – 599 YARDS

It is a sign of an immaculately tended course when visitors mistake your first teeing area for a practice green. As an antidote to Britain's more rugged golfing experiences, *The Oxfordshire* is a pristine American-style parkland course that offers the ultimate tactical challenge across water. Aptly described by the club as a 'thinking golfer's dream – and a thoughtless golfer's nightmare', this monster par-five requires the player to carry as much water as he dare – often with disastrous consequences!

After a sturdy drive, the player has the choice of two completely different routes – a ferocious 200-yard carry across the lake to the left-hand fairway or a more sedate but longer trip to the right of the water. This was the route members were choosing on the day of our visit but, after your second shot, 'right-siders' are still likely to face a testing short-iron to a green peppered with the course's characteristic white sand bunkers.

TWO ROUTES TO THE 17TH GREEN

THE OXFORDSHIRE – OVERHEAD OF THE 8TH

The 17th has had some illustrious casualties. During the 1996 Benson and Hedges International Open, the wind gusted up to 50mph contributing to Pardraig Harrington's score of 13 on this hole.

The four lakes of *The Oxfordshire* feed the course's 1300 sprinklers. The largest, sitting in the middle of the course, provides a spectacular hazard for the 10th, 11th and, most notably, the 359-yard par-four 8th where the green balances on a narrow peninsula, inviting a second shot over the ornamental island with its solitary tree.

> ### THE FOUR LAKES FEED THE COURSE'S 1300 SPRINKLERS

THE OXFORDSHIRE – THE 8TH GREEN BACK TO THE FAIRWAY

PAINSWICK

GLOUCESTERSHIRE,
GL6 6TL

5TH 'CASTLE'
PAR 3 - 114 YARDS

5TH TEE

Set on the public land of the Cotswold Hills, *Painswick's* 18 holes may only measure 4831 yards in total but they are amongst the most amazing 4831 yards of any golf on the planet. Practically a theme-park of British landscapes, the course opens up like a story book. It takes a player across Painswick Beacon, with its views to the Welsh mountains, through Iron Age hill forts, escarpments, quarry works, tree-lined parkland and, at the magnificent downhill 16th, finally releases him back onto the village green.

When playing to the 4th green, with the hill fort looming, you get the distinct impression that the course has reached a mysterious dead-end with nowhere logical to go. Having found the 5th tee, shrouded in trees, it takes a moment to realise what one is being asked to do. Facing the player are two giant folds of land that rise up to encircle the green sitting in the basin at the top. Assuming you make it over the top, there is some margin for error on the right but a hook will see the ball end up in wispy grass and rocks in the middle of the fold to the left.

OVER THE RAMPARTS AT THE 5TH

PAINSWICK – THE HOLLOW IN THE 11TH

PAINSWICK – FROM THE ROAD TOWARDS THE 16TH TEE

PAINSWICK – FROM THE 10TH GREEN BACK OVER THE STRANGE KNOLLS

Situated on the Cotswold Way itself *Painswick* swarms with walkers, particularly on Sundays when play is not possible. There are no bunkers but the remarkable undulations in the land provide more than enough challenges. The course features a number of vast pits, one with the remains of a tree at the 1st and a quarry to play over from the 14th tee (harrowingly named 'Gallows'). A 20ft hollow waits to catch anything right at the 6th, or the 11th.

The land around the par-three 10th 'Postern' consists of a series of grassy mounds that hardly look as if they are of this world. The scene looks strangely out of place for a southern English landscape. The green, over a ridge, is the only place to land. *Painswick* is essentially a 'there and back' layout; though for the final three holes, there is a detour almost into the village itself with the 16th and 17th carefully picking their way through the minor roads back towards the clubhouse. Definitely a course for straight-hitters, *Painswick* has to be England's foremost hidden masterpiece.

42

PLEASINGTON

BLACKBURN,
LANCASHIRE,
BB2 5JF

7TH
PAR 5 - 527 YARDS

Multi-levelled greens are commonplace but this rolling Lancashire course has a highly unusual multi-levelled fairway. Your tee shot is a drive over some rough up an incline but there is an entirely separate fairway that is yet to come in the valley below. If you can manage a drive of 230 yards with some fade on it, the ball should find the downslope to the lower level and run, satisfyingly, straight down the hill. But even if you cannot achieve that distance, a second shot from the high fairway gives the chance to launch a wood gloriously towards the green.

LOOKING BACK TO THE TOP FAIRWAY ON THE 7TH

PLAY DOWN FROM THE HIGH FAIRWAY TO THE LOW

PLEASINGTON – 16TH OVER THE BEECH TREES

Pleasington's par-three 16th (154 yards) calls for plenty of height off the tee as the green is set within a sunken dell protected with beech trees, that with their canopies in summer can tower to 80ft high. Clearing them is the first problem – stopping the ball the other side, the next.

Pleasington is split by the railway line that serves Blackburn and Burnley. *Peover*, Cheshire, with its schoolboy smirk-inducing pronunciation, is split down the middle by the M6.

PLEASINGTON – THE 16TH GREEN IS IN A DELL

PRESTWICK

SOUTH AYRSHIRE,
KA9 1QG

17TH 'ALPS'
PAR 4 - 391 YARDS

Home of the first Open Championship in 1860, in which the course's original 12 holes were played three times in a day, *Prestwick* has seven of the greens still intact within the current eighteen-hole layout. The bunker at the 17th instils as much fear as it did nearly 150 years ago and remains difficult to beat as Britain's most imposing greenside hazard. The base of the sand-trap is completely flat and comparatively hard-surfaced, in contrast with modern bunkers that tend to have softer sand within an elliptical base. It does not help that the approach shot to the 17th is completely blind over a range of dunes.

BIG TROUBLE AT THE 17TH IF YOU MISS THE GREEN

Prestwick has a natural and charmingly unkept feel, with a number of feature hazards notably the 'cardinal' bunker at the par-five 3rd (482 yards), a huge swathe of sand built up with sleepers that straddles the fairway. The course was only taken off the Open rota because it could not contain the large crowds.

THE ADDINGTON – A FLIGHT OF STAIRS TO GET INTO THE BUNKER ON THE 3RD

Though bunkers can be ranked methodically by their dimensions, some have gained notoriety for their positioning alone. There is nothing particularly exceptional about the actual sand trap on the 3rd at *The Addington*, Surrey, but since it lies at the bottom of a vast chalk pit that has to be crossed by one of the course's characteristic wooden bridges, it must be a contender for the most vicious bunker in the land.

45

PYRFORD

SURREY,
GU22 8XR

6TH
PAR 3 - 127 YARDS

LITTLE BUT SAND BETWEEN TEE AND GREEN ON THE 6TH

The scariest looking hole-planner you could ever set eyes on belongs to *Pyrford*, near Woking. Though the word 'pyre' is actually derived from the Greek for fire, it is water that dominates this modern Peter Alliss/Clive Clarke layout. There are 23 acres of water hazards which impinge on 17 of the 18 holes.

But the single hole that does not have water is quite exceptional. This short par-three has almost nothing but a sprawling bunker between the tee and the green.

Note the little touch of the two plants neatly arranged in its middle.

At the 6th, with what could be classed as a small beach to carry, you might be inclined to play very long to be safe. But to add another complication, the green slopes severely from back to front leaving a nasty downhill putt if you go longer than pin high.

PYRFORD – A BIT SHORT AT THE 6TH

PYRFORD – WATER ALL THE WAY DOWN THE 9TH FAIRWAY

PYRFORD – THE FINAL CARRY OVER THE WATER AT THE 9TH

On closer inspection, the design of *Pyrford* is not quite as punishing as it looks as there are a variety of tee positions that ease the task for those of lesser experience. Although menacing to the eye, the many lakes do not require drastically long carries. But the club's signature hole still has many finding a watery grave. The 9th (592-yard par-five) skirts its way to the left of the drink. At some point you have to decide when you feel up to the final carry over the water to the green. Being *Pyrford*, the green has a bunker at the front edge and the putting surface is anything but level.

THE SCARIEST LOOKING HOLE-PLANNER YOU COULD EVER SET EYES ON

REDDISH VALE

STOCKPORT,
CHESHIRE,
SK5 7EE

18TH 'THE HILL'
PAR 4 - 353 YARDS

Set out in the valley of the River Tame, *Reddish Vale* takes advantage of a number of natural ravines and gullies. The 18th plays back up the hill to the manor house in which the club has its home. The flag is clearly visible from the tee but, once positioned on the fairway, the second shot becomes blind. With trees both sides, the hole forms a perfectly framed natural boulevard. *Reddish Vale* is in a county boundary 'grey area'. The club plays in the Cheshire Union of Golf Clubs though, some may argue that it lies within Greater Manchester.

A LAST EFFORT UP THE HILL BEFORE THE CLUBHOUSE

STOKE PARK CLUB – 7TH; A MODEL FOR *AUGUSTA'S* FAMOUS 12TH

Reddish Vale was designed in 1912 by Alistair MacKenzie. He was the architect for the *Augusta National* Course, USA, home of the US Masters, as well as two other world renowned courses *Cypress Point* and *Royal Melbourne*. Arguably the most famous golf hole in the world, the par-three 12th at *Augusta* is perhaps also the most copied. There are many British holes similar to it, some designed by MacKenzie himself.

The essential component of the azalea-clad *Augusta National* 12th (155 yards) is a tiny green – only nine yards deep at its smallest point – protected by a creek and two bunkers, one at the front (which has recently been widened) and another at the back.

RIDDLESDEN

WEST YORKSHIRE,
BD20 5QN

6TH

PAR 3 - 115 YARDS

IN SUMMER AVOID THE TREE CANOPIES ON THE 6TH

West Yorkshire's rolling hills are ideal territory for unusual golf holes – explaining why the county is so well represented in our collection.

Stepping onto the 6th tee at *Riddlesden*, moorland opens up to the north. But, searching in all directions, there is a conspicuous lack of a fairway to aim for. It is only when glancing around that the newcomer becomes aware of a lonely green 160ft below to the south in a quarry, a gaping pit produced by excavations for the Leeds Liverpool Canal. "They can't seriously expect me to hit down there" is the usual reaction. Firing through a dark, dense clump of trees, this is hit-and-hope with a nine-iron territory. You can forget about anything short – there is no path directly from the tee to green.

As advised by the Health and Safety Executive, there is a sign on the 6th tee warning of the sheer drop.

THE 6TH PLAYING OVER THE QUARRY

The one forgiving aspect of *Riddlesden's* short layout is that you do not have to play back up the quarry later. But having negotiated the 6th, another hole uses the feature to unnerving effect. The par-three 15th (112 yards) plays semi-blind to a tiny green protected by a rock face at the front and a deep pit to the back.

The par-three 18th (160 yards) plays straight over the 17th green and is obstructed by a tree to the left at 80 yards. But any over-compensation for the tree risks rattling a drive through the clubhouse window to the right of the green. Specialised toughened glass has been fitted to try and limit the impact, though the roof tiles come in for a lot of punishment.

Putting a ball through any car window is rare; putting it through your own car window is something else. But in 1996, Mr J Simpson, then club captain of *Riddlesden*, hooked his shot from the 18th tee into the car park in the valley, shattering his rear window.

RIDDLESDEN – SHORT DOWNHILL **15**TH

RIDDLESDEN – A FISH-EYE VIEW OF THE **18**TH PLAYING DOWN TO THE VULNERABLE CLUBHOUSE

29

ROYAL NORTH DEVON

WESTWARD HO!
DEVON,
EX39 1HD

4TH
PAR 4 - 349 YARDS

THE SLEEPERED 'CAPE BUNKER'

With a bit of pre-planning it is possible to attempt to play over Britain's duo of most incredible bunkers in the same day when in the south-west. Whilst the legendary hill of sand at *St Enodoc's* 6th is famed for its vast height, the sleepered 'Cape Bunker' on the 4th at *Royal North Devon* is staggering because of its width. To clear it requires a tee shot of 150 yards not excessive with today's hi-tech equipment but, even for a confident driver, it is a formidable sight from the tee, stretching at least 60 yards across the entire fairway. With the old feather balls displayed in the club's golfing museum, the hole must have been fearsome beyond belief.

Royal North Devon is the oldest club in England still playing over its original course. Founded in 1864, today's layout was largely constructed in 1908 – but the feel of the course is like stepping back centuries in time. Over the years the 'Cape Bunker' has been neatened. Pictures from the early 1900s reveal it was a rougher, sprawling affair, spilling out everywhere like a mini-beach in the middle of the course.

> THE 'CAPE BUNKER' IS STAGGERING DUE TO ITS WIDTH

ROYAL NORTH DEVON – NOT THE GREATEST SPOT TO FIND OFF THE TEE AT THE 4TH

The great British links courses all feature characteristically undulating fairways – but *Royal North Devon's* are perhaps the granddaddies of ancient playing tracts. The 6th has a particularly gnarled fairway, the humps and dips of which tend to suddenly seem larger when you land on or in them – meaning players get lots of practice of shots above and below their stance.

The key hazard of the three holes after the turn is the man-sized sea rushes. So sharp are their tips that, it has been known for older style golf balls to become impaled on them. To make the 10th fairway, a carry of over 150 yards is needed to clear these swaying rushes.

The exclamation mark attached to the end of the name of the village of Westward Ho! is a trivia quiz classic. The use of the punctuation is accepted as the name's correct form.

THE UPS AND DOWNS OF *ROYAL NORTH DEVON'S* 6TH

85

ROYAL ST GEORGE'S

SANDWICH,
KENT,
CT13 9PB

4TH
PAR 5 - 497 YARDS

The question 'which is the biggest bunker in Britain?' is not easily answered; it depends on your definition of 'biggest' and, possibly, your definition of 'bunker'. For some, *St Enodoc's* 'bunker' on its 6th is really a huge hill of sand, though the distinction is less than clear.

Recently the 4th at *Royal St George's* has been extended with the enormous bunker now lying 230 yards from the back tee. This monstrous beast is almost certainly the deepest in Britain. At 20ft high, the slatted face towers alarmingly in front of anyone who finds the bunker.

ATTEMPTING TO ESCAPE FROM BRITAIN'S STEEPEST BUNKER

ROYAL ST GEORGE'S PRO DEMONSTRATING THE TEXTBOOK BUNKER RECOVERY

Very occasionally, bunkers can be placed as an act of benevolence. During the exceptionally dry summer of 1975, the second green at *Church Stretton*, Shropshire, began playing so fast that one unfortunate golfer managed to send a putt off the green, down a hill, and through a fence to out of bounds. The club kindly put a bunker next to the green to prevent any recurrence.

The largest surface area of any British bunker is on the par-five 4th at *The Oxfordshire*, aptly named 'Hell's Half Acre'. The 'Sahara' bunker stretches threateningly across the entire width of the fairway at 315 yards. The minimum carry to avoid it is 70 yards.

Royal St George's is considered amongst the world's premier tournament venues having hosted, in 1894, the first British Open Championship to be played outside Scotland. Though many will have seen the BBC coverage – most recently the 2003 Open – the stubbornly two-dimensional nature of television pictures does not always do justice to the peaks and troughs of the course. Up close, it is a fiendishly undulating layout winding its way through the sand dunes of Sandwich Bay.

One of the side effects of the professionals being able to hit the ball so far in recent years is that features such as this amazing bunker are effectively taken out of play. Lesser mortals might struggle to clear it, but Tiger would need to go to pieces in order not to sail his drive clear over the top.

THE OXFORDSHIRE – 'HELL'S HALF ACRE' AT THE 4TH

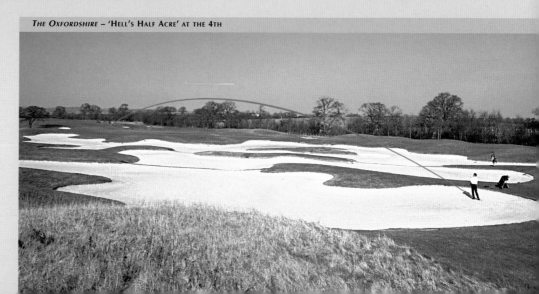

25

ROYAL TARLAIR

MACDUFF,
ABERDEENSHIRE,
AB44 1TA

13TH 'CLIVET'
PAR 3 - 152 YARDS

A NERVE-SHREDDING SHOT TO THE HEADLAND AT 'CLIVET'

ROYAL TARLAIR – LOOKING BACK TO THE PRECIPITOUS TEE AT THE 13TH

O f all Britain's Royal clubs, this cliff top parkland course in north east Scotland has the most reasonable green fees and possesses a sea-hole to rival any in the world. The scene from the 12th tee is breathtaking but the golfing challenge that awaits is one of those 'pit-in-the-stomach' moments.

The green is perched on a headland below, angled in such a way that it looks like it is about to slide down the cliff. Between you and safety is a vast gorge. The mind can only ruminate on what lies over the back of the green. In fact, it is worse than it looks with another sheer drop down to the beach. When, or if, you make it, there is the compensation that *Royal Tarlair's* greens are in superb condition all year round.

The premier championship course in Wales, *Royal St Davids*, Gwynedd, had a bit of a false start in assuming its Royal title. Edward VII, then Prince of Wales, granted his patronage in 1897 and, in 1901, the club starting using the 'Royal' prefix having wrongly been advised that this was part of the package. In 1909, its Royal status was officially conferred but the powers that be registered their displeasure by writing: "The Secretary of State regrets that the Club should have wrongfully adopted the title in 1901".

21

SALISBURY AND SOUTH WILTS

NETHERHAMPTON,
WILTSHIRE,
SP2 8PR

18TH
PAR 3 - 163 YARDS

THE PIT AT THE 18TH

Many 18th holes play directly at the clubhouse, causing a few butterflies for a player, fearing he could be the one to disturb the secretary's afternoon tea by rattling a long iron onto his desk. This predicament applies to *Salisbury and South Wilts*' finisher. The green is just 15 yards away from the building but it is the trouble you could encounter on your way that makes this hole so special.

Just in front of the tee lies a massive pit, 85 yards across and 30ft deep. Its ability to unnerve players is so great that few first-timers ever make the green in one. In 2002, a society of 25 had to draw lots for the 'nearest-the-pin prize' as not a single player managed to get their tee shot on the green.

The flag visible in the picture is *not* that of the 18th hole; it is actually a 20ft flagpole that stands outside the clubhouse. The real, and considerably smaller, flag is just visible in our picture to its right.

A tree-lined Roman road catches many stray drives to the right of the fairway on the 491-yard par-five 16th.

SALISBURY AND SOUTH WILTS – THE 16TH WITH A ROMAN ROAD

SHISKINE

**BLACKWATERFOOT,
ISLE OF ARRAN,
KA27 8HA**

3RD
'CROWS NEST'
PAR 3 - 122 YARDS

THE NEAR VERTICAL TEE SHOT AT THE 3RD

SHISKINE – LOOKING BACK FROM THE 3RD GREEN

Just about everything at *Shiskine* defies belief including perhaps our photo on the facing page of its 'short' 3rd. It really does play into the heart of the gigantic rock face. Somewhere in the middle of the edifice is a green – though newcomers often have to clamber up first to confirm their suspicions. It is without doubt the steepest upward shot in Britain – 90ft almost vertically upwards. Overlooking the Mull of Kintyre, the course is so unique that it does not bother with the usual convention of having nine or 18 holes, instead it offers 12.

The course has a host of blind shots to greens, meaning that a variety of devices signal to the next party that the green is clear. The 3rd has a flag, the 11th a bell and, most unusually, a mechanical lever that you pull on the 7th green sending a signal back to the tee. There are ravines, plunging tee shots, burns, gorse and a mild, sunny climate. Its 10th is named 'Paradise' for its 360 degree panoramic views – such a favoured spot for one couple that they were married on the tee.

Having endured the uphill hardship of the 3rd, players are rewarded at the amazing 4th 'The Shelf' (137 yards) playing back down to sea level from perhaps the ultimate elevated tee.

SHISKINE – 4TH TEE

SILVERDALE

LANCASHIRE, LA5 0SP

13TH 'PLATEAU'
PAR 4 - 312 YARDS

GREEN BALANCED ON THE ROCKY PLATEAU

SILVERDALE – PATH LEADING UP TO THE **13**TH GREEN

with the best drive in the world it is impossible to avoid the 25ft high wall of limestone rock that has to be overcome to reach the green on top of the plateau. When completing this treacherous hole, a peal of a sturdy bell signals that the green is clear.

The limestone on the course is not only a scenic hazard, but it also enables water to drain away very easily allowing the course to remain open in winter when others are battling against standing water. The 8th requires a drive over Myers Dyke where, if you are very lucky, you may get a glimpse of an otter.

Silverdale frequently heads lists of the friendliest club in the country.

Having possessed an unusual twelve-hole layout until 2002, *Silverdale Golf Club* has been extended to the full eighteen. Lying on the southern boundary of the Lake District, the course is built amongst a series of limestone rocks. The 13th is reasonably plain sailing from the tee across a valley – but even

SILVERDALE – BACK ALONG THE FAIRWAY FROM THE **13**TH GREEN

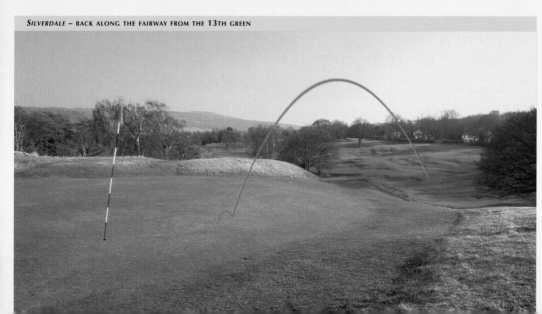

SILVERDALE – THE GREEN-SIDE BELL AT THE **13**TH

90

SLEAFORD

LINCOLNSHIRE,
NG34 8PL

12TH
PAR 3 - 138 YARDS

OVER THE EVERGREENS IF YOU CAN

Seve Ballesteros once commented that there was nothing to fear when playing through the canopies of trees because they mostly consisted of air. If you fancy testing the theory out, *Sleaford's* 12th is the perfect place. The idea here is to try and clear the copse of pine trees and land swiftly on the other side though, inevitably, many are forced to take the low route if they duff their shot from the tee. Being evergreen trees, the shot is just as tough in the depths of winter.

With so many heavily wooded courses in Britain, it is perhaps surprising that there are not that many holes where trees 'deliberately' obstruct the fairway. On the par-four 16th at the public course of *Altrincham*, Cheshire, the route is entirely blocked, requiring a heroic carry to the green beyond whilst avoiding the brook that runs through the wood.

Sleaford is remarkably well-drained and rarely suffers in winter weather but one of the more incredible rule debates occurred during a hideously wet spell in early January 2003 when the bunkers became submerged in ice and water. A senior member, well known for his slavish adherence to the rules, argued to the other members of his party that the habit of lifting a ball without penalty from a water-filled bunker was not, strictly, following the letter of golfing law.

SLEAFORD – LOOKING BACK OVER THE TREES TO THE 12TH TEE

At the 15th, our friend found himself in a partially frozen bunker and, despite protestations from the others, insisted on attempting a 'legal' escape, so avoiding a one-shot penalty. Dropping the ball onto a few particles of sand peeping up over the water, he edged out onto an area of ice to take up his stance.

With expert comic timing, the ice gave way sending him, still faithfully clutching a sand-iron, into the freezing, watery hollow. With equal inevitability, he refused to withdraw tactically to the warmth of the clubhouse and played out the final three holes soaked to the skin.

ST ANDREWS

FIFE,
KY16 9SF

17TH 'ROAD'
PAR 4 - 461 YARDS

One of the idiosyncrasies of the golfing scene is that the Old Course at *St Andrews*, the most prestigious championship layout in the world, is actually a public facility. This does not mean that you can jump out of the car and straight onto the first tee at the home of golf but the six courses owned by the St Andrews Trust are accessible to players of all abilities. The Old Course is fully booked for at least six months in advance though, in June and September, there is a ballot system in operation.

The Old Course has simply evolved over time, a version of the game having been played there 600 years ago, so no single designer can take credit. One of its unique facets is its vast double-greens where the outward and inward holes play to the same putting surface. This results in putts of over 100 yards – longer than some short par-threes.

ST ANDREWS IS ACTUALLY A PUBLIC FACILITY

CUT THE CORNER AT THE 17TH BY GOING OVER THE HOTEL

The tee at the 17th is tucked away round a corner with the out of bounds St Andrews Hotel on the right. The direct line to the green plays straight over the one-storey part of the building. No current day designer would dare propose such a layout – nor would they consider the incredible positioning of the 17th green, tucked away against a stone wall dividing the course from a public road in the town.

If you are lucky enough to get a tee-off time at the Old Course, don't commit the sin of walking onto the 1st and triumphantly take a few lashing practice swings. The starter does not appreciate people taking chunks out of the sacred turf and a casual warm-up could result in you being asked to leave the course before you have even started.

Although *St Andrews* is the spiritual home of golf, it is the East Lothian coast to the south that probably has the highest density of courses of any area in the world. The epicentre of all this golfing activity is the village of Gullane (pronounced Gull-un). The village, with a population of just 2500, is home to five golf courses. From the height of the 17th at *Gullane* itself, the mass of East Lothian fairways is visible in all directions. To reinforce the dominance of the game, *Gullane's* first tee is squarely in the centre of the village along with a children's course and a Golf Museum.

Also within the village boundary is *Muirfield*, host of many memorable Open Championships. Home of the Honourable Company of Edinburgh Golfers, the club has a reputation for exclusivity, having famously turned ex-PGA champion Payne Stewart away on a members' day. Indisputably one of the world's finest courses, visitors are now permitted on Tuesdays and Thursdays. However, it is not Britain's most expensive club for visitors – that accolade goes to the Old Course at *Sunningdale*, Berkshire, where a round will set you back a cool £120.

THE HEIGHTS OF *GULLANE* WHERE GOLF DOMINATES THE VIEW

GULLANE – PLAYING OUT OF THE VILLAGE

3

ST ENODOC

ROCK,
CORNWALL,
PL27 6LD

6TH
'HIMALAYAS'
PAR 4 - 378 YARDS

SAND HILL LOOMING AT THE 6TH

ST ENODOC – FROM THE TOP OF THE SAND HILL LOOKING TO THE GREEN

In terms of the most spectacular natural hazard on a British golf course, *St Enodoc's* Himalayan sand hill wins with something to spare. From the 6th tee on the Church Course, the 80ft monster bunker rises up in the middle of the fairway. The green lies another 160 yards further on amongst a batch of sand dunes. There is a narrow strip of land to the left that, in theory, it is possible to pitch onto but otherwise there is no easy route apart from up and over the sand hill. It hardly needs to be said but, once stuck there, most amateurs are lucky to make any sort of recovery shot – such is its vicious steepness. There is the small consolation of the views from the top of the hill.

St Enodoc perches on the North Cornwall coast – a classic though, at 6243 yards, not overly long, links course with rolling fairways and numerous natural sand hazards. Far from being a big-hitters' paradise, *St Enodoc* is a course for those who do not leave their golfing brains in the clubhouse.

The nearby village of Rock has been dubbed 'Chelsea sur-mer' for its large (and prosperous) ex-London population.

ST ENODOC – ABOUT THE WORST PLACE TO END UP ON A BRITISH GOLF COURSE

ST ENODOC – SUNKEN CHURCH NEXT TO THE 10TH GREEN

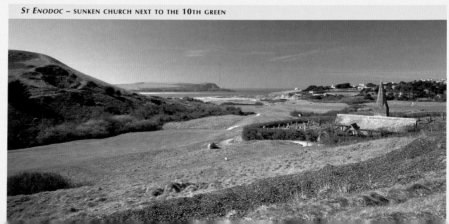

48

STONEHAVEN

COWIE,
ABERDEENSHIRE,
AB39 3RH

13TH 'RED MAN'
PAR 4 - 252 YARDS

Having trains rumbling through the middle of your golf course does not help concentration for those difficult shots but it does provide a good shop window for passing commuters. The Scottish east coast line crosses a bridge over a ravine, just north of the town of Stonehaven. Intrigued passengers often return to the club to play a round having glimpsed the course from the train window.

RAIL PASSENGERS GET A GOOD VIEW OF THE DRIVE OVER THE RAVINE

STONEHAVEN – BACK ACROSS THE RAVINE ON THE 15TH

The 13th is a classic carry over the heather-clad plunge to a fairway that continues slightly uphill the other side. Overall, *Stonehaven* can feel that it plays uphill all the way though, at only 5103 yards, it is no slog. The slopes you really have to worry about are on the dramatic fairways that run along the 100 metre cliffs of the bay, where everything seems to lean towards the abyss making them tricky to hold.

Stonehaven turns back on itself with the 15th playing the other way over the gully, this time as the par-three 15th 'Gully Cup' (161 yards). It is practically all carry over its entire distance and, with the wind in the wrong direction, has a reputation for being unplayable with an iron.

One of the course's hazards was not intended by the designers. A crater that comes into play for those who stray off the first and second fairways was made when a German bomber dropped a shell on the course in August 1940. It is now dubbed 'Hitler's bunker'. The 2nd tee balances on a headland, requiring a carry across the cliff edge. If you dare look down you might see one of the porpoises or dolphins that surface in Stonehaven Bay.

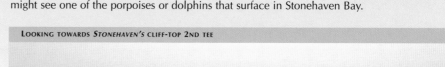

LOOKING TOWARDS *STONEHAVEN*'S CLIFF-TOP 2ND TEE

STRATHENDRICK

DRYMEN,
STIRLING,
G83 8EL

8TH 'BROON'S BRAWEST'
PAR 3 - 178 YARDS

BLIND FROM THE 8TH TEE

STRATHENDRICK – THE FIRST OBSTACLE ON THE 8TH IS A MINI-ABYSS

STRATHENDRICK – DOWN THE SLOPE TOWARDS THE GREEN ON THE 8TH

B lind shots, and particularly blind par-threes, tend to incite moans from amateur golfers. All that neck-craning and hopping up and down to see if the green in front is clear can slow the pace of a round considerably when you do not have the eager ball-markers that the pros rely on.

Here at *Strathendrick's* 8th there is a marker post the other side of a gorge, with its neat little bridge taking players across. With a long-iron you can give the ball a hearty thwack from the tee and, if straight, it should find the downslope and roll somewhere in the vicinity of the green, hiding in the valley below.

Across the water from *Strathendrick*, on Scotland's sparsely populated west coast, lies the Isle of Bute, home to a golf course with the most unusual layout in the country. Devotees of logic problems can try to disentangle how *Port Bannatyne* manages to create an eighteen-hole round from 13 actual holes. After completing 12 holes, players go back to the 1st and play holes one to five again. The finishing par-three 18th is an entirely different hole to the preceding 12 thus giving the club a unique total of 13 holes.

> **BLIND SHOTS, AND PARTICULARLY BLIND PAR-THREES, TEND TO INCITE MOANS FROM AMATEUR GOLFERS**

57

SUTTON BRIDGE

SPALDING,
LINCOLNSHIRE,
PE12 9RQ

5TH

PAR 5 - 535 YARDS

Changes in fairway elevation are commonplace but not quite on the scale of the gigantic step upwards in the fairway of this par-five. The tee is on a raised area to the right of the fairway. After their first two shots, the uninitiated may find themselves scratching their heads when looking around for somewhere to aim a third shot. The fairway seems to just end as players are confronted by a 15ft high wall. Though it seems unlikely at the time, you are supposed to fly one straight over and up onto the higher section where, 20 yards further on, the green is to be found.

THE DOCK WALL TO SURMOUNT ON THE 5TH

Sutton Bridge, founded in 1914, is set within an abandoned dock basin. The dock's site was some 500 yards long and 150 yards wide. Its original walls now form an integral part of this nine-hole course which, with its mature willow and poplar canopies, provides a superb setting for golf.

Walls come into play on seven holes, including the par-four 7th where one crosses the fairway at right angles, providing a stiff test in order to clear it from the tee.

The original dock basin was not in use for long. Almost as soon as its construction was complete, it was struck by an engineering catastrophe. At the time, three ships were docked on the site now occupied by the course. The walls began to collapse, causing alarm as workers managed to get the ships into safer waters. The land remained unused for the next 33 years until locals had the idea of laying out a golf course on the vacant 35 acres.

Secretary of *Sutton Bridge* Norman Davis recalls the story of two members who provided their own sighting mechanism at the 5th. Accompanied on their round by their young son, they would position the pram (with the baby still in it) further up the fairway to indicate the best route to the 5th green.

The Committee swiftly ended the practice.

SUTTON BRIDGE – A BARRIER TO PROGRESS ON THE 5TH FAIRWAY

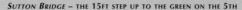

SUTTON BRIDGE – THE 15FT STEP UP TO THE GREEN ON THE 5TH

TAIN

HIGHLAND,
IV19 1JE

11TH 'ALPS'
PAR 4 - 380 YARDS

Tain is frequently overlooked as a great links course but, with the sea on one side and mountains on the other, its setting is amongst the most inspiring the Highlands can offer. It is a course to pick and think your way round. Humps, bumps and odd undulations frustrate golfers everywhere but *Tain* has a couple of particularly extreme fairway-hills in play.

Guarding the 11th green are two vast mounds, with a marker post indicating the best line of fire for your

THE 'ALPS' AT THE 11TH FROM THE TEE

THE APPROACH OVER THE HUMPS

approach shot. *Tain* was established in 1890 and, in 1917, underwent a somewhat radical redesign whereby the old 10th, 11th and 12th 'sea-holes' were effectively completely reversed – so the tees became the greens and vice versa. This meant that the hills of the current 11th used to have to be cleared from the 12th tee.

Celebrity spotters are in their element in the fashionable nearby town of Dornoch. One particular Scottish actor known to frequent the area appeared in perhaps the most famous golfing movie scene of all time. Our photo of the grand clubhouse of *Stoke Park Club*, Buckinghamshire, should stir a few celluloid memories as it featured prominently in the golfing scene from the film. To see the clubhouse as it appeared in the film, turn to page 195.

Whenever you see a golf course on TV, it is a good bet that it is the super-lush layout at *Stoke Park Club*. The course recently featured in the BBC drama 'Manchild' starring Nigel Havers and scenes from 'Bridget Jones's Diary' were shot at the lake and in the clubhouse.

TAIN – LOOKING BACK FROM THE 11TH GREEN

STOKE PARK CLUB – THE LOCATION FOR WHICH FAMOUS GOLF MOVIE SCENE?

96

TEMPLE

MAIDENHEAD,
BERKSHIRE,
SL6 5LH

10TH
PAR 3 - 246 YARDS

SUNKEN GREEN ON THE 10TH

TEMPLE – PLAYING INTO AN AMPHITHEATRE ON THE **10TH**

surrounds the amphitheatre. It was certainly not 'purpose-built' for the golf course. Some say it was a cockfighting pit, others an ancient meeting place for knights.

___

The answer to our picture puzzle is that *Stoke Park Club* was the setting for the golfing scene in the James Bond film 'Goldfinger' where archvillain Oddjob helps Goldfinger cheat his way to victory against 007. He memorably gets his comeuppance in a scene in which he patches himself into the national grid whilst trying to retrieve his bowler hat.

At 246 yards from the back tee, the 10th is a mammoth three-shotter. At just 15 yards longer, the course's finishing hole makes par-four status. But if your ball pitches on or near the 10th green, you are almost home and dry – it is unlikely to find its way anywhere else. The putting area is framed by an almost perfectly circular amphitheatre. The surrounding land, including the area between tee and green, is relatively flat, only helping to emphasise the pit into which you have to aim. The depth of the punchbowl is actually more than it looks in our picture. On the facing page, the flag pole peeping over the hill is 10ft tall.

As is often the case with these types of features, a certain amount of legend

GOLDFINGER DUBIOUSLY TRIUMPHS AGAINST BOND AT *STOKE PARK CLUB*

97

TRADITIONS

PYRFORD,
SURREY,
GU22 8UE

9TH
PAR 4 - 384 YARDS

THE STEP UP IS JUST AT THE RIGHT LENGTH TO CATCH DRIVES

The village of Pyrford, in the commuter belt of Surrey, is home to two of the country's most distinctive American-style courses. Like *Pyrford* itself, *Traditions* is the brainchild of Peter Alliss and it is packed with his charac-teristic design features that make picking a single hole rather difficult. On some holes the fairways are punitively tight and most of the greens are heavily protected requiring well-aimed lobs to overcome a host of bunkers and water hazards.

TRADITIONS – NOT WHERE YOU WANT TO LAND ON THE 9TH

In his BBC commentaries, Peter Alliss rarely mentions the courses he has designed. But whenever the subject of testing greens comes up, keep an ear out for how many times he mentions the Dukes Course at *Woburn*, Buckinghamshire, the lavish and very tough Charles Lawrie-designed layout that for many years hosted the British Masters.

> ## THE 9TH HAS A PARTICULARLY TAXING FEATURE IN THE MIDDLE OF THE FAIRWAY

TRADITIONS – THE OBLIGATORY APPROACH OVER WATER ON THE 18TH

The 9th has a particularly taxing feature in the middle of the fairway. At 214 yards from the tee, the fairway moves to another, higher, level. The 15ft step is built up with chunky railway sleepers. Its positioning is somewhat mean, as a good drive risks getting stuck behind it for your second. At least there is no sand at its base.

Amongst *Traditions'* many testing features is one of the narrowest fairways in the land. The fairway on the par-four 4th narrows to 20 yards wide in places with trees lining each side. The 16th is an 'S' shaped par-five, doglegging to the left and then, for your approach to the green, requiring an almost 90 degree turn to the right.

But it would not be an American-style course without an 18th over water. The finishing 402-yard par-four challenge has a testing carry over a lake.

37

VERULAM

ST ALBANS,
HERTFORDSHIRE,
AL1 1JG

17TH
PAR 3 - 135 YARDS

A HIGH LOB IS NEEDED ON THE 17TH

VERULAM – LOOKING BACK TO THE 17TH TEE

CRICKET AND GOLF SHARE THE SAME LAND AT *HARPENDEN COMMON*

Verulam is the spiritual home of the Ryder Cup. Samuel Ryder was the captain here when the competition started in 1927. Today the course has plenty of out of bounds areas but its feature hazard comes on the 17th where a road bisects the course. Increasingly the minor road is being used as a short cut to the town and has to be protected by netting. At 135 yards, it is no mean feat to confidently lob over the traffic and a ball from the tee that is not dead straight will get tangled up in the bushes. Go long and you are left with a nasty chip back down a sharp slope. Consequently, we are inclined to vote this as the ultimate beginners' nightmare hole.

At nearby *Harpenden Common*, the golf club shares its 3rd fairway with Bamville Cricket Club. The cricketers have priority so, on Sunday afternoons between May and September each year, the golf course is reduced to 17 playable holes. The 540-yard par-five 3rd plays straight over the wicket. From the tee, aiming at the cricket club's pavilion is considered to be the best line of fire. The tee lies beyond the cricketers in our picture. Our kind poseurs are on the fairway 'illegally' but they help to illustrate the line of fire into the green. Until recently the 3rd was a much shorter hole, playing to a green that was virtually on the cricket pitch itself but was moved to its new position away from the Sunday afternoon cricket crowds.

WARREN

DAWLISH WARREN,
DEVON,
EX7 0NF

7TH

PAR 4 - 332 YARDS

HOW MUCH OF THE ESTUARY DO YOU RISK TAKING ON?

One of Britain's most unusual geophysical features, the tiny strip of land between the English Channel and the Exe estuary, is home to *Warren's* 7th tee. The tee shot, facing west, is played with the estuary hugging the fairway on the right. It is just a question of how much of the estuary you want to take on. Most aim for a concrete irrigation building but for the optimistic there is always the option of going for the green in one mighty hit, although the 235-yard carry is too far for most to contemplate. It is quite possible to end up on the estuary

beach so recovery shots from the sand are quite routine. You do not want to overshoot the fairway as the rough to the left is punishingly heavy.

And that is only the situation at low tide. When the tide comes in, much of the strip of land becomes submerged. The elevation of the tee allows the hole to continue to be played but with water stretching out on all sides, the 7th is the closest British golfers can get to playing a shot from in the sea itself.

WARREN – BEACHED GOLFER ON THE 7TH

right around the clubhouse to an unusually narrow green, 40 yards long but just 20 yards wide – and an even more unusual position, backing onto Dawlish Warren railway station as little as 14ft from the actual track.

Warren seems to be a popular name for golf clubs. There are two other British courses called *Warren*, one in Wallasey and one in Woodham Walter, Essex.

THE 18TH GREEN IS 14FT FROM THE RAILWAY TRACK

When visiting *Warren*, our photographer was approached by a fellow snapper with a hearty "what have you got?" After being on a different wavelength for a few moments, it was clear that he was more interested in the area's rare birdlife than rare golf holes. *Warren* falls completely within a National Nature Reserve (explaining its popularity with 'twitchers') and is home to a variety of protected plant and bird species. But, golf and conservation can go hand in hand. The course is managed with the environment in mind as there are few modern tending techniques employed, allowing the club to offer golf 'as it used to be'.

The 399-yard par-four 18th is a noteworthy railway hole. The tee lies on an island, playing blind over a copse of trees. The second shot doglegs left to

WARREN – 18TH BACKING ONTO DAWLISH WARREN RAILWAY STATION

WHITBY

**LOW STRAGGLETON,
NORTH YORKSHIRE,
YO21 3SR**

16TH
PAR 4 - 479 YARDS

Whilst many holes featured in our collection will be permanent features for many years to come, *Whitby's* amazing holes, played over a gorge, are under threat. The east coast is fighting a battle against erosion, with the result that at least a section of the course is in some danger of being lost to the forces of the North Sea. The ravine over which both the 7th and the 16th play is the public footpath to the beach.

THE **16TH** PLAYING OVER THE PATH TO THE BEACH

vulnerable sea-holes. At its narrowest point, the 6th fairway is now only 36ft wide and shrinking at a rate of 5ft a year.

With a lot of dangerous drops on the course, the cliff tops are not the place to get stuck in fog. The club sounds a foghorn when visibility is reduced. Anyone on the course is expected to stop playing immediately.

The club can be praised for its policy of encouraging a diverse membership – not always a priority for many British clubs – and is keen to boost its membership from ethnic minorities and the disabled.

> **THE CLUB SOUNDS A FOGHORN WHEN VISIBILITY IS REDUCED**

WHITBY – 7TH THREATENED BY EROSION

WHITBY – 7TH TEE

The 16th has a 100-yard carry over the ravine. A bridge that over the years has had its original wood replaced by concrete takes you across to the fairway. Surprisingly, since it is a public area, the ravines are an integral part of the course and not out of bounds – so if you make a mess of it from the tee you can find yourself thrashing around below.

The other play over the ravine comes at the par-four 7th (446 yards) with its tee close, and getting closer, to the edge of the seafront cliff. *Whitby* has secured a grant from the lottery commission to fund a project aimed at relocating the most

WIGAN

GREATER MANCHESTER,
WN1 2UH

18TH
PAR 4 - 445 YARDS

Until recently this was a nine-hole course, somewhat hampering the club's jocular attempts to persuade the Royal and Ancient to host the British Open at *Wigan*. The new 18th requires a carry of over 160 yards to clear a gorge that has been carved out by Arley Brook. The ravine is 40ft deep with tall trees either side limiting the margin for error. A rustic bridge takes players over onto the fairway the other side.

THE TEE SHOT NEEDS TO GET AS FAR UP THE BANK AS POSSIBLE

WIGAN – MIND THE TREE ON THE APPROACH TO THE **18**TH GREEN

In theory, a perfectly hit drive onto the upslope leaves you with a clear shot at the green. But many struggle around the right-hand dogleg and end up having to play over or through a giant beech tree that stands menacingly close to the putting area.

As if the carry from the tee at *Wigan's* 18th was not enough to worry about, there is a depression just to the right of the fairway caused by a Second World War bomb. Many British golf clubs remained open during the war years, requiring special rules in the event of enemy attack. The Secretary of *St Mellons*, Cardiff, drafted 'combat rules' including the provision that "a player whose stroke is affected by a simultaneous explosion of a bomb or shell, or by machine gun fire, may play another ball from the same place. Penalty one stroke". How generous.

On the final day of the Olympics in 1936, the German team was leading the British golfing team and Adolf Hitler was due to present the prize which included a fir tree. On hearing that the British had won the match, Hitler turned his car around, leaving the prize-giving to a subordinate. One of the recipients of the British team was Arnold Bentley from *The Hesketh*, Merseyside, where the fir tree was planted. At the outbreak of war, the tree became the focus of members' disdain. To demonstrate their displeasure, golfers routinely relieved themselves on the poor specimen. The 'pissing tree', as it became known, still stands to this day but is reported to be 'a very peculiar shape'.

15

WILLOW VALLEY

BRIGHOUSE,
WEST YORKSHIRE,
HD6 4JB

14TH
'DANIEL'S DARE'
PAR 4 - 424 YARDS

APPROACH OVER WATER ON THE **14TH**

WILLOW VALLEY – THE FAIRWAY LAKE TO OVERCOME AT THE **10TH**

The approach from the east, on the M62 from Manchester, snakes its way through the barren wilderness of the Pennines. Having seen the landscape they have just driven through, motorists tempted by *Willow Valley's* huge billboard at Hartshead Moor Services might imagine that golf in the area could be a gloomy affair.

But *Willow Valley* is actually a recently built American-style series of two senior courses, a junior course and a driving range. No fewer than 15 lakes were created for the complex and a staggering 50,000 trees and shrubs, not to mention eight tonnes of bulbs, were planted.

The largest of these lakes almost totally surrounds the 14th green, leaving a tough approach over water to a mere 30 yards of green. The land that links the green to the fairway is only seven paces wide. To catch nervous second shots, a bunker cruelly waits just short of the lake. There is even one to the rear of the flag on the island itself.

The name of the 14th on the South Course, like all at *Willow Valley*, was chosen with local history in mind. 'Daniel's Dare' is a reference to the author of 'Robinson Crusoe', Daniel Defoe, who travelled the area in the early 18th century. The 9th, skirting very close to the north carriageway of the M62, is named 'Almost Halfway' not, as golfers might imagine, a reference to their progress around the course but because this point on the M62 is close to halfway between Liverpool on the west coast and Hull on the east.

Another lake comes into play in an unusual way on the massive 623-yard par-five 10th. Water tends to protect greens but rarely does it suddenly impinge in the middle of the fairway. The lake is unlikely to trouble the drives of most club golfers but the 50 yards of water lie in just the area where long-hitters would be hoping to reach. The hole has another claim to fame – perhaps the greatest discrepancy between a mens' and ladies' tee in the country. From the back tee the men cop for the full 623 yards but the ladies are asked only to negotiate 344 yards – their tee lying just short of the lake. They also get the use of a wooden 'ladies shelter'.

Water comes into play on 11 of the South Course's 18 holes though, sometimes, it is not the only hazard. A rock face and a strategically placed tree also guard the 188-yard 6th.

Before it opened in 1969, contractors working on the M62 were concerned that livestock could find their way onto the carriage-way. In a series of bizarre experiments to determine the design of the barriers, sheep were studied to discover how high they were able to jump. So it is not by chance that the fences are 4ft 10in high.

WILLOW VALLEY – PAR-THREE **6TH** OVER THE LAKE

26

WINDERMERE

BOWNESS-ON
WINDERMERE,
CUMBRIA,
LA23 3NB

8TH
PAR 3 - 130 YARDS

The south coast has the 5th at *Isle of Purbeck*; the far north, the 10th at *Shiskine*. To complete a set of great scenic holes, this one is just about in the middle of the British Isles, 600ft above sea level within the boundaries of the Lake District National Park.

Windermere's 8th plays from an elevated position. Behind lies Morecambe Bay and in front the often snowcapped Lakeland peaks. The green is on practically the same level as the tee, but between the two is a deep, forbidding hollow with rocks scattered around the upslope to the green. Pitching the ball onto the plateau putting surface is one thing – making it stay there, quite another. Not much sticks to this green as everything slopes away from its middle.

THE SLOPING GREEN OF THE 8TH

LAKELAND HILLS PROVIDE THE BACKDROP FOR THE 8TH HOLE

WINDERMERE – **BLIND OVER THE ROCKS AT THE 6TH**

WINDERMERE – **6TH GREEN**

At 5132 yards, *Windermere* is not a big-hitter's course but rather demands the player to carefully negotiate some unusual English golfing terrain, with tough bracken, hillocks and rocks coming into play. The par-four 6th (361 yards) has one of the club's nerve-wracking but exhilarating blind shots – 160 yards over a rocky face to a characteristically humpy fairway with a lake to avoid on the second shot.

Well-known local residents in the past include William Wordsworth and children's writer Beatrix Potter whose characters have been trade-marked, so we are not at liberty to refer to the overbearing duck and foppish rabbit.

WOODHALL SPA

LINCOLNSHIRE,
LN10 6PU

5TH
PAR 3 - 150 YARDS

Frequently awarded the honour of the top inland course in Britain, *Woodhall Spa* ends our collection with the most punitively guarded green you may ever encounter. On the Hotchkin Course, the scene around the 5th's putting area is golf's equivalent of the 'Gates of Hades'. Anything short or to the right is destined for the torment of the huge bunker that hooks its way around the green. Another beast catches long approaches. Individually, though not the absolute deepest in the country, they are contoured in such a way as to make escape as testing as possible. The club is rightly proud of its bunkers' somewhat notorious status and makes every effort to keep them sturdily built up.

TROUBLE EVERYWHERE AT THE 5TH GREEN

Along with *Ganton*, North York-shire, *Woodhall Spa* is one of the few clubs that slavishly follow the line that landing in a bunker should result in some sort of penalty or hardship. From the end of the Second World War, British bunkers have become less punishing and, fearing the commercial implication of putting off a player of average ability, tend to be designed with aesthetics in mind.

Woodhall Spa's cavernous bunker at the 5th allegedly claimed a non-golfing victim. Someone, who, for an unknown reason, drove their car across the course and ended up bunkered, vehicle and all.

DISLEY – SMOKE SHAFT ON THE 1ST

NOTTS – PAUSE AT THE 'HOLYWELL'

The 1st fairway at *Disley*, Cheshire, has one of the unluckier places to drive a golf ball. At around 160 yards, there is a smoke shaft of the old Midland railway tunnel that runs beneath the course. Though the target area is small, it has been known to collect a few slices.

As a refreshing halfway house for the stressed golfer, the heathland Championship course of *Notts* has a natural spring on its 8th where players can drink from a metal cup. But if the frustrations of golf make you yearn for something a little stronger, the 12th at *Nefyn and District* has a path down the cliff to the less demanding atmosphere of the Ty Coch Inn.

IF IT ALL GETS TOO MUCH, DITCH THE CLUBS AND HEAD DOWN TO THE PUB

REVIEW OF RANKING RESULTS

Nobody associated with the book had heard of *Eyemouth* before embarking on the project but it soon became clear that its death-defying 6th over the North Sea was going to be ranked number one with something to spare. From *Eyemouth*, it is only five miles down the east coast to *Magdalene Fields*, ranked 18, another incredible play over the sea.

Of our top 20, there were 12 coastal courses with water features of one sort or another accounting for many of the highly ranked holes. The geographical split was eccentric to say the least. North-east Scotland is the world centre of the game – so where did six of the top ten come from? ... south-west England!

St Enodoc won the battle of the bunkers at number three with *Woodhall Spa's* horrendous sand-trap ranked 19th. The highest placed green feature was *North Berwick's* giant hollow at 52. Some clubs may have achieved a higher ranking if we had picked a different hole to feature. *The Oxfordshire* might have been disadvantaged in this respect because we chose its unusual double fairway hole instead of its Sahara bunker. Similarly *Crondon Park* may have suffered somewhat, as we could not ignore its enormous 18th. So this hole was featured rather than one of its more photogenic. We kept changing our mind over *Dartmouth's* feature hole – but either the 3rd or the 18th would have made our top 10, and the 9th on its par-three course is not to be missed either.

The biggest 'surprise packages' were *Willow Valley*, that picked up a steady number of votes to creep in at 15, and *Salisbury and South Wilts*, who only missed the top 20 by one place. The highest ranked unusual feature was *Brocket Hall's* ferry at 23, pursued by *Great Yarmouth and Caister* playing across the racecourse which came in at number 32.

Our 12 week sprint round the country generated over 7,000 photographs. In the process the authors and photographers developed their 'pet' courses – the ones that conversation would always turn back to. Mark Davidson Fildes found wandering around in the clouds of a deserted *Dufftown* a positively spiritual experience. Adam Godfrey crowed about *Shiskine* and the purring Ferrari of all courses, *The Oxfordshire*. Vanessa Strowger developed a strong affinity to *Riddlesden* and *Cullen*, and everyone had to endure Geoff Harvey continuously dreaming up superlatives to describe *Painswick*.

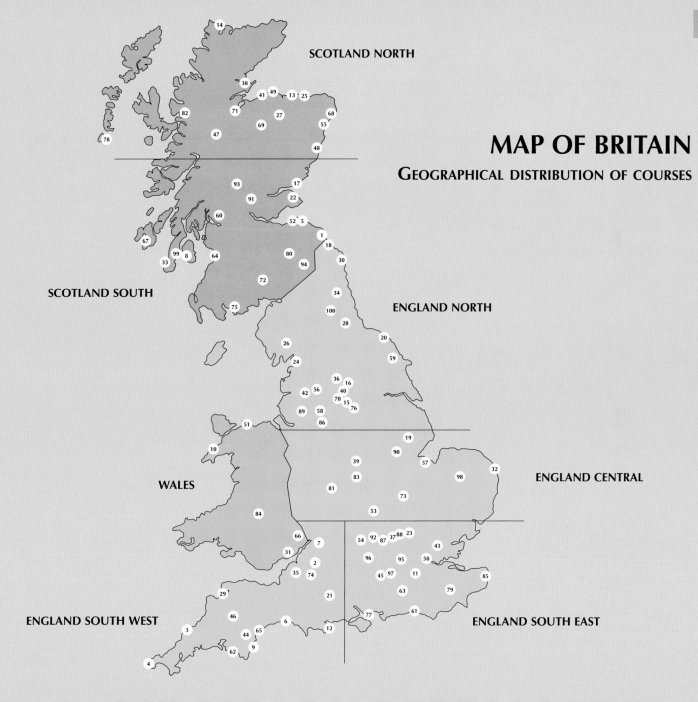

MAP OF BRITAIN

GEOGRAPHICAL DISTRIBUTION OF COURSES

SCOTLAND NORTH

SCOTLAND SOUTH

ENGLAND NORTH

WALES

ENGLAND CENTRAL

ENGLAND SOUTH WEST

ENGLAND SOUTH EAST

GEOGRAPHICAL LISTING AND INDEX

NEARLIES, MAYBES AND HAS-BEENS

In the course of writing 'Britain's 100 Extraordinary Golf Holes' one of our featured clubs went out of business so, for the time being, it's RIP *Arbory Brae*, Dumfries and Galloway. Laid out on 25 acres of ground, the holes were a faithful recreation of the original nine-hole course that lay dormant for over forty years; the idea being that, by playing the course with old-style hickory clubs, players could get a genuine taste of the Victorian golfing experience.

The most enthusiastic and detailed submission we received was from Peter Parr, Chairman of the British Minigolf Association, who nominated the 15th hole at Whiterock Gardens, Hastings as Britain's most extraordinary minigolf hole.

With $10,000 for the World champion and a clutch of European professional players, minigolf is treated far more seriously in some circles than its popular image of toddlers swinging clubs helplessly at 1:20 scale windmills. Possibly because of its association with childhood seaside holidays, as adults many are close to fanatical in their adoration of the game. www.miniaturegolf.com features a collection of pictures showing hundreds of minigolf holes around the world.

With so much material pouring in there were a lot of tough decisions on which courses to include. Looking back on the project some courses that for a long time we assumed would be included were squeezed out at the last moment. In this

ARBORY BRAE – NOW GOING BACK TO NATURE

category *Polkemett Country Park*, West Lothian and *Edenbridge*, Kent, were particularly unlucky.

For a golf book, remarkably few golf balls were actually hit by the team in the course of its production. But photographer Adam Godfrey decided he couldn't resist the opportunity to have a crack at *Eyemouth*. The trajectory on the photograph above shows the result.

Prize for best poseurs goes to Simon and Chrissie at *Windermere*, who made the 8th look almost routine by both firing their tee shots within feet of the flag.

www.extraordinary-golf.com

ACKNOWLEDGEMENTS

A big thank you to all the people at golf clubs around the country who submitted information, photographs, and stories including:

Abernethy – Bob Robbie
The Addington – Bob Hill
Aldwickbury Park – Alan Knott
Arbory Brae – Alfie Ward
Baildon – Mr J Cooley, Louise Milne
Bamburgh Castle – Alan Patterson
Barra – Joe McLeod
Bath – Mr S Ware
Bigbury – Martin Lowry
Boat of Garten – Paddy Smyth
Boxmoor – Jim Newark, Geoff Donovan
Braemer – John Pennet
Bramshaw – Bob Tingey
Brancepeth Castle – Brian Cullen
Branston – Vanessa Archer
Bridport & West Dorset – David Parsons
Brighton & Hove – Phil Bonsall
Brocket Hall – John Wells
Brora – James Fraser
Cambridge Meridian – Ingrid van Rooyen
Cams Hall Estate – Steve Wright, Chris Geest
Cape Cornwall – Mike Waters, Una Handley, Ernie Keddie
Carradale – Dr Robert Abernethy, Susan Maxwell, Geoffrey Page
Castlefields – Fred Tolley, Mr J Briggs
Charnwood Forest – John Tooley, James Clarke
Chart Hills – Mary Millen
Chiltern Forest – Bob Clift
Clayton – Mr Ward, Paul Brooksbank
Collingtree Park – Jamie Hammond, Geoff Pook
Crondon Park – Stuart Fox, Paul Cranwell
Cruden Bay – Rosemary Pittendrigh
Cullen – Ian Findlay, Chris Hayes, Kate Bain
Dainton Park – Mike Cayliss

Dartmouth – Jamie Warr, Tony Chappel
Dewsbury District – Mr Dando
Dewstow – John Harris
Disley – Diane Bradley
Dufftown – Marion Swann
Dukes Meadows – Scott Margetts
Durness – Lucy MacKay
Erewash Valley – Joe Beckett
Eyemouth – Mary Gibson, Andrew Renton
Fereneze – Graham McCreadie
Fort Augustus – John Morgan, Mr A Burnett
Fulford Heath – Mrs M Tuckett, Kim Blake
Galashiels – Mr Young
Ganton – Bob Woolsey
Gatehouse – Keith Cooper
Glen – Kevin Fish
Gorleston – James Woodhouse
Great Yarmouth & Caister – Robert Peck
Green Haworth – Tony Alveston
Gullane – Mr Owram
Harpenden Common – Peter Clarke, Diane Monroe
Heaton Park – John Mort
Hemingford Abbots – Ian Quinn, Ms S McCabe
The Hesketh – Martyn Senior
Hirsel – Stuart Galbraith
Hopeman – Jim Fraser
Hounslow Heath – Dave Carter, Louise Acres
Ingol – Derek Smith, Alan Read
Isle of Purbeck – Mrs J Robinson
Jedburgh – Keith Swailes
Killin – Trevor Taylor, Shona Milligan
Kirby Muxloe – Brian Woodcock
Llandrindod Wells – Robert Southcott, Mike Williams
Loch Ness – Neil Hampton
Lochcarron – Alastair Beattie
Long Ashton – Bob Williams

Lundin Ladies – Marion Mitchell
Lyons Gate – Mr Pires
The Machrie – Bob Hogben, Ian Brown
Machrihanish – Thomas Newlands, Anna Andersen
Magdalene Fields – Malcolm Lynch
Mannings Heath – Steve Murphy
Manor House – Mark Stevenson
Matfen Hall – David Burton
Miniature Golf – Peter Parr
Moffat – Mr JW Mein
Monmouth – Peter Tully
Moray – Steve Crane
The Old Musselburgh Links – Ian Sills
Muthill – Jim Elder
Nefyn & District – Barry Owens
New Forest – Mrs B Shaw
Newburgh On Ythan – Roger Bruce
Norfolk GC Club – Tony Varney, Mike De Boltz
North Berwick – Norman Wilson
North Wales – Gordon Downs
Northcliffe – Ian Collins
Notts – Ian Symington, Brian Noble
Okehampton – Clive Yeo
Orsett – Derek Howe, Amanda Hughes
The Oxfordshire – Jennifer Daniels, Richard Moan, Timothy Street
Painswick – Norman Hindmarsh
Piltdown – Peter De Pinna
Pleasington – Mike Trickett
Port Bannatyne – Beryl Burnett
Pyrford – Tristan Hall
Reddish Vale – Bryan Rendell
Riddlesden – Colin Stead, Anthony Heap, Mike Neild
Royal North Devon – Robert Fowler
Royal St George's – Mr A Cook
Royal Tarlair – Caroline Davidson
Salisbury & South Wilts – Pat Clash

Sandhill – Bob Platts, Valerie Wistow
Shiskine – Fiona Crawford
Silverdale – Keith Smith
Sleaford – Terry Gibbons
St Enodoc – Mr T Clagett, Josh Greenaway
Stoke Park Club – Andrew Copsey, Sophie Freer
Stonehaven – Bill Donald
Strathendrick – Pete Marrison
Surbiton – Chris Cornish
Sutton Bridge – Norman Davis
Tain – Kathleen Ross
Teign Valley – Mike Daniels
Temple – Keith Adderley
Top Golf – Dawn Cremin
Traditions – Tony Healy
Verulam – John MacGuire
Warren – Tim Aggett
Wellingborough – Andy Horn
Whitby – Duncan Russell
Wigan – Ted Walmsley
Willow Valley – Julian Haworth
Windermere – Mr Moffat, Simon Fildes

Other information sources:
Club web pages. golf-europe.com. AA Guide to Golf Courses 2003.

We also owe thanks to the following for their support and help in making this book possible:

Carole Bates, Sally and Dan Germain, John Glover, Kevin Hughes, Jonathan Oliver, Statoil, David Swain, Linda Strowger, Nigel Trotter.

PICTURE CREDITS

Adam Godfrey
Front cover, 5, 6, 7, 9, 10, 11, 19, 20, 21, 24, 25, 26, 27, 28, 29, 30, 31, 32, 33, 38, 39, 40, 41, 43, 44, 45t, 48, 49, 50, 51, 54, 55, 60, 61l, 62, 63, 64, 65, 66, 67, 70, 71, 73, 77b, 80, 81, 82, 83, 84, 85, 88, 89, 90, 91, 92, 93, 100, 102, 103t, 105bl, 109b, 110, 111l, 116, 117t, 120, 121, 122, 123, 126, 127, 128, 129tl, 129bl, 130, 131, 132, 133, 138, 139, 142, 143, 144, 145, 146, 147, 150, 151, 152, 153t, 154, 155b, 156, 157tl, tr, 158, 159, 164, 168, 169, 170, 171, 174, 175, 176, 177, 178, 179, 180, 181, 183, 184, 185, 188, 189, 190, 191, 193b, 194, 195t, 200, 201, 202, 203, 206, 207, 211tl, 216, 217, 222.

Mark Davidson Fildes
4, 8, 12, 13, 14, 15, 16, 17, 18, 34, 35, 36, 37, 46, 47, 52, 53, 56, 57, 58, 59, 61r, 74, 75, 78, 79, 96, 98, 99, 101, 104, 105t, 106, 107, 112, 113, 117b, 124, 125, 129tr, 129br, 134, 135, 136, 137, 140, 141, 148, 149, 161, 162, 163, 166b, 167, 172, 173, 186, 187, 192, 193t, 196, 197, 198, 199, 204, 205, 208, 209, 211tr, 217b, 221.

Geoff Harvey
94, 95, 105br, 109t, 111r, 157bl, 166t.

Eric Hepworth
42, 108, 119, 160, 182, 210.

Scottish Viewpoint
22, 23, 72.

Hazel Groome
86, 87.

Barbara Berkowitz
76, 77t.

Alex Ingram
114, 115.

© Stoke Park Club
97, 165, 195b.

Alan Strowger
35r.

Glyn Satterley
118.

Chris Cornish
103b.

Andy Horn
153b.

The Golf Business Limited
155t.

Alan Dudley
45b.

Listed by page number and where necessary location on the page.
Key: b bottom, c centre, l left, t top